Sustainability
in Interior Design

Published in 2012
by Laurence King Publishing Ltd
361–373 City Road
London EC1V 1LR
Tel +44 20 7841 6900
Fax +44 20 7841 6910
E enquiries@laurenceking.com
www.laurenceking.com

A catalog record for this book is available from the British Library

ISBN 978 185669 8146

Commissioning editor: Philip Cooper
Senior editor: Melissa Danny
Designer: John Round Design

Printed in China

Picture credits:

Front cover Koby Cottage, Albion (US) by Garrison Architects.

Back cover Section showing stack ventilation. Drawing: Nicholas Hacking.

Title page Yeshop fashion boutique in Athens (Greece) by dARCH Studio.
Photo: Vassilis Skopelitis.

Opposite "Soft" seating by Molo made of unbleached, recycled-content
Kraft paper. Photo: Molo.

Sustainability
in Interior Design

Siân Moxon

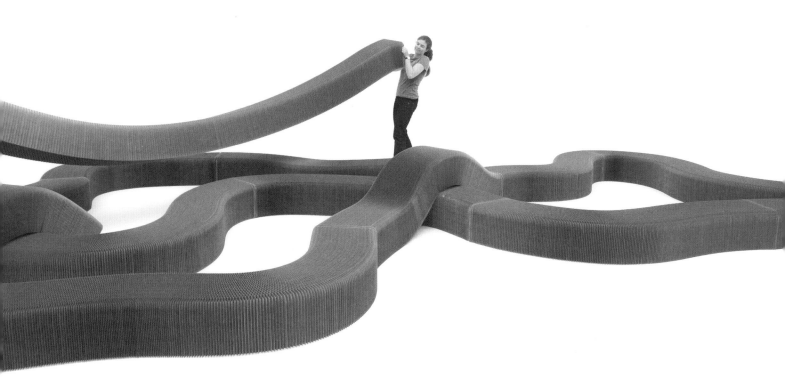

Laurence King Publishing

Contents

6   **INTRODUCTION**

8   **CHAPTER 1: CONTEXT**

10   **Introduction**

10   **The problems**
10   Climate change
11   Step by step: Climate change
12   Diminishing resources and biodiversity
12   Waste
12   Allergies and stress
12   Water scarcity
13   Population growth
13   The construction industry

14   **Sustainability and the role of interior designers**
18   Step by step: Design impact

19   **History forgotten**
19   Traditional buildings
21   Modernist design

24   **Relearning**

26   **Disregarding preconceptions**

29   **Why this book is required**

30   **CHAPTER 2: A SUSTAINABLE APPROACH**

32   **Introduction**

32   **Embracing compromise**
32   The unsustainable nature of construction
32   The scale of the problem
32   Knowing where to begin
33   Approaching compromise

36   **Considering consequences**

38   **Asking the right questions**
39   1. What is the purpose of the project?
42   2. How long will the interior be required?
44   3. What energy and water systems are appropriate?
45   4. What materials are appropriate?
47   5. What construction methods are appropriate?
49   6. How will the space function?
52   7. What will happen to it when it is no longer useful?

53   **Assessment**
54   Case study: LEED assessment
56   LEED
56   BREEAM
56   Ska Rating
57   NABERS
57   Green Star Australia
57   Green Globes
58   BEAM
58   CASBEE
58   DGNB
59   Case study: Green Star assessment
60   Step by step: Assessment process

Related study material is available on the Laurence King website at
www.laurenceking.com

62	**CHAPTER 3: KEY ISSUES TO UNDERSTAND**
64	**Introducing the key issues**
64	**Energy**
64	Impacts of energy use
66	Approaching low-energy design
67	Step by step: Low-energy design
68	Passive design
72	Energy efficiency
74	Renewable energy systems
75	Energy assessment
76	Case study: Low-energy design
78	**Water**
78	Impacts of water use
78	Approaching water-conserving design
79	Step by step: Water-conserving design
80	Passive design
80	Water efficiency
82	Water reuse and recycling
83	Flood protection
83	Water assessment
84	**Materials**
84	Impacts of materials
86	Step by step: Ceramic tile life cycle
88	Step by step: Carpet life cycle
90	Approaching sustainable specification
91	Step by step: Sustainable materials specification
92	Specification checklist
93	Reduce
95	Reuse
96	Recycle
97	Renewables
98	Case study: Choosing materials
100	Materials assessment
102	Choosing materials
102	Base materials
103	Flooring
104	Finishes
105	Fabrics
106	Furniture
106	Further information

107	**Construction methods**
107	Impacts of construction methods
109	Approaching sustainable construction
110	Reduce
114	Reuse
115	Recycle
116	Furniture construction
118	Case study: Sustainable construction
120	Step by step: Flat-pack furniture
122	**CHAPTER 4: PUTTING SUSTAINABILITY INTO PRACTICE**
124	**Introducing the projects**
124	**Temporary projects**
134	Case study: Nothing advertising agency
136	Case study: Yeshop boutique
138	**Flexible projects**
150	Case study: The Elgar Room
152	Case study: Howies store
154	**Long-term projects**
172	Case study: Design Council headquarters
174	Case study: Renctas store
176	**CONCLUSION**
180	**Glossary**
180	**Further reading**
182	**Websites**
186	**Picture credits**
187	**Index**
192	**Acknowledgments**

Introduction

It is time for change in the field of interior design. With our daily lives saturated with talk of climate change, interior designers need to join other construction industry professionals in tackling this and other environmental issues. Building has a significant impact on the environment, and interior projects are no exception. Fortunately, interior designers—with their focus on renovation projects, lighting, and materials—are well placed to instigate change.

Change can be effected by a combination of relearning lessons from the past and embracing new technologies. There is much inspiration to be taken from traditional buildings and iconic designers from the past few centuries, whose good design inadvertently produced sustainable results. Meanwhile, new products, such as LED lighting, prefabricated components, and veneers, can be exploited to complement basic sustainable design principles. The results need not conform to an "eco" style: sustainability can simply be part of any good design.

It is vital that interior designers first consider how to approach designing sustainably. This involves overcoming potential barriers to environmentally conscious design, considering the consequences of design decisions, and knowing what questions to ask during the design process. Designers can even opt to use a formal assessment system to ensure a rigorous approach.

To inform their approach, interior designers must understand the principles underpinning sustainable design and how these should influence their choices of energy and water systems, materials, and construction methods. They must also gauge how to apply their knowledge to different types of interior project—whether temporary, flexible, or long-term—to ensure the most sustainable outcome possible.

A band of pioneering designers around the world already leads the way. Their work demonstrates how sustainability can be incorporated effectively in interiors, without compromising aesthetics or design quality. This book aims to equip and inspire other designers to follow suit.

The book is set out in four chapters that guide interior designers through the sustainable design process:

Chapter 1, **Context**, introduces the principal environmental issues, and explores how today's interior designer can learn from historic examples of sustainable design. The chapter also counters unhelpful preconceptions about sustainable design and affirms why this book is a useful tool for interior designers.

Chapter 2, **A Sustainable Approach**, suggests how to go about designing to achieve sustainable results. This involves being willing to compromise, foreseeing the consequences of design choices, asking oneself key questions, and using design assessments.

Chapter 3, **Key Issues to Understand**, explains how to select energy and water systems, materials, and construction methods to limit an interior's environmental impact. The chapter sets out valuable sources of independent guidance for more detailed research.

Chapter 4, **Putting Sustainability into Practice**, presents a selection of exemplary recent interiors from around the world. These are categorized into temporary, flexible, and long-term projects, and show how their designers have incorporated sustainability to suit the project type.

Case studies and step-by-step illustrations are used throughout the chapters to clearly demonstrate the issues being discussed.

The book closes with a glossary of important terms and suggestions for further reading, including contact details for featured designers, manufacturers, and organizations.

Opposite
In this visualization of Nature Café La Porte in Amsterdam (Netherlands), RAU architects depict natural materials such as bamboo dominating the interior, showing a sustainable approach during the design process.

Above
Yeshop fashion boutique in Athens (Greece) by dARCH Studio features reused materials and low-energy lighting. The walls are made from layered cardboard sourced from packaging.

Above
Incubation retail unit in Melbourne (Australia) by Matt Gibson Architecture + Design is built for flexibility, with reconfigurable hinged panels and the ability to be subdivided.

CHAPTER 1 CONTEXT

10 INTRODUCTION

10 THE PROBLEMS

14 SUSTAINABILITY AND THE ROLE
OF INTERIOR DESIGNERS

19 HISTORY FORGOTTEN

24 RELEARNING

26 DISREGARDING PRECONCEPTIONS

29 WHY THIS BOOK IS REQUIRED

Introduction

Interior designers can relearn important lessons from the past to understand how to create sustainable designs. This chapter will explain the environmental issues we face today, review historic examples of sustainable design, and discuss how the interior designer can apply past principles to address today's issues. This chapter also dispels prevailing myths surrounding sustainable design and confirms why this book is required by contemporary interior designers.

The problems

We face unprecedented challenges today. The issues of climate change, diminishing resources and biodiversity, waste, allergies and stress, and water scarcity have come to light in recent times and increasingly affect our lives. These environmental issues are reaching crisis point and are, rightly, a major topical issue. All of these issues have been compounded by population growth, magnifying human impact on the planet, and all will have disastrous consequences if they continue unchecked. The construction industry is a major contributor to environmental damage, which interior designers are well placed to mitigate through championing sustainable design.

This section explains the key environmental issues and their implications. It then describes how the construction industry, and specifically interior design, contributes to them.

Climate change

Climate change, often described as global warming, is perhaps the most alarming of the environmental issues we face. Human activities—such as burning fossil fuels for energy and transportation, cutting down trees for wood or agriculture, and allowing waste to decompose in landfill sites—have produced excess greenhouse gases, particularly carbon dioxide (or carbon) and methane. As a result, quantities of these gases in the atmosphere have soared to unprecedented levels, intensifying the natural greenhouse effect. The greenhouse effect is the process by which naturally occurring greenhouse gases—such as water vapor, carbon dioxide, and methane—absorb radiation from the Earth's surface, keeping our atmosphere warm and our planet habitable. But excess greenhouse gases strengthen this effect. They build up in the atmosphere, forming a thick "blanket" around the Earth that gradually heats it up, causing overall warming and affecting climate patterns.

It is important to stress that, according to most mainstream climate scientists, there is overwhelming evidence that climate change is happening now and

Carbon emissions per person per year (tons)

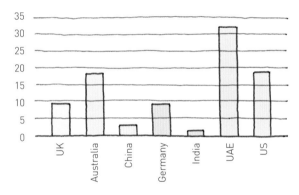

Graph comparing carbon emissions per person for key countries. (Source: US Department of Energy, based on UN statistics.)

Share of world's carbon emissions (%)

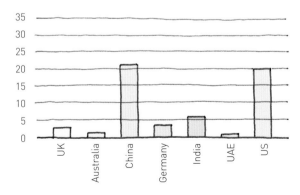

Graph comparing share of total world carbon emissions for key countries. (Source: US Department of Energy, based on UN statistics.)

STEP BY STEP CLIMATE CHANGE

The following diagrams explain how man-made climate change happens:

1 The process begins with human activity, including burning fossil fuels, felling trees, manufacturing, storing waste in landfill sites, and driving vehicles. As the human population grows, so this activity increases.

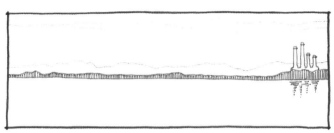

2 These actions release excess greenhouse gases, such as carbon dioxide, methane, and hydrofluorocarbons, which accumulate in the atmosphere.

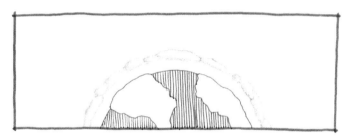

3 As a result, a "blanket" of greenhouse gases forms around the Earth, strengthening the natural greenhouse effect and trapping too much heat within the atmosphere.

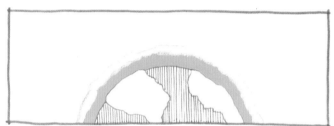

4 The Earth consequently warms up, causing changes in Earth's climate and rising sea levels, affecting humans and unbalancing ecosystems.

is caused by human activity. The Intergovernmental Panel on Climate Change advises that climate change is unequivocal, and manifested by an increase in global air and sea temperature, widespread snow and ice melting, and rising global average sea level. The 12 warmest years in recorded history were 1995 to 2006, and the Earth has warmed by 32¾°F (0.4°C) since the 1970s. The average extent of Arctic sea ice has decreased by nearly 3% every decade, while global average sea level has risen at an average rate of around ⅛ in (3mm) per year since 1993.

The effects on our weather patterns are already apparent. In recent years, precipitation in the northern hemisphere, drought in the southern hemisphere, and extreme weather events such as heatwaves and heavy rain are believed to have increased. The number of cold days has decreased, while the number of hot days has increased. There is also evidence of climate change affecting natural systems and human activities: for example, crop seasons and disease patterns.

It is interesting to note that developed countries have the highest carbon emissions per person: the United Arab Emirates, then the US, then Australia being the top three. But the emerging developing countries dominate the highest total carbon emissions, China being the top offender and India ranked third—with the US remaining in second place.

If we fail to act, greenhouse gas emissions are projected to increase by between 25 and 90% by 2030 from 2000 levels, causing warming of 32½°F (0.2°C) per decade. This would cause increased coastal flooding; wetter, warmer winters and dryer, hotter summers in the northern hemisphere; and more frequent storms, drought, and heavy rainfall worldwide. Such changes would affect humans, as well as wildlife and ecosystems.

Unsightly, polluting mountains of waste are a routine by-product of our lifestyles.

"Our world has enough for each person's need, but not for his greed."
MAHATMA GANDHI

CONSUMING RESOURCES

"If everyone lived like a North American we'd need five planets to live on. If everyone lived like a European we'd need three planets to live on."

One Planet Living, a global initiative based on ten principles of sustainability developed by BioRegional and WWF

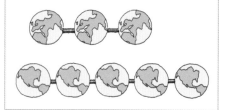

Diminishing resources and biodiversity

Humans are using up natural resources—including forests, fossil fuels, and minerals—faster than they can be replaced by nature, creating an unsustainable situation. Some resources, such as fossil fuels and stone, are finite or replenished only over millennia. This means that once they are used up, many of the resources we depend on will not be available for future generations. Valuable fossil fuels —including coal, oil, and natural gas—are steadily running out, leading to rising energy prices, and concerns over energy security when their supply is under the control of particular countries. Loss of forests and other habitat for wildlife is diminishing biodiversity (the variety of living things on Earth), with certain species and the ecosystems that depend on them becoming vulnerable or extinct.

If we allow this trend to continue, there will be scant natural resources for future generations to use for survival and enjoyment, bringing human conflict. Wildlife and wilderness will steadily decline, unbalancing ecosystems and diminishing access to the natural world for human pleasure and relaxation.

Waste

Many of our production methods are inherently wasteful, as is our habit in the West of throwing things away and buying anew. Our waste takes up space in landfill sites. Here it either degrades to release pollutants, including greenhouse gases, into the soil, water, and atmosphere; or, in the case of plastics, remains indefinitely, taking up space in unsightly waste "mountains" or islands of detritus at sea that are harmful to wildlife. In 2001, landfill sites produced a quarter of the UK's methane emissions.

Allergies and stress

We spend 90% of our time indoors, where off-gassing from chemicals in finishes and furniture exposes us to allergies, asthma, and Sick Building Syndrome. US studies show indoor levels of air pollutants to be almost three times higher than outdoor levels. Meanwhile, our hectic urban lifestyles, disengaged from the calming surroundings of the natural world, often cause stress.

Failing to address these issues will result in diminished human health and well-being.

Water scarcity

We are using more and more water in the developed world, both for personal use and within the products we use. In the UK, water use has been rising by 1% every year since 1930: daily use now totals 40 gallons (150 liters) per person for essential needs, and more than 900 gallons (3,400 liters) when one factors in the embedded water in all the products we consume. Besides being wasteful, there is a significant amount of energy associated with treating and delivering potable water, which in turn contributes to greenhouse gas emissions and therefore climate change. In the US, the energy used to provide clean water represents 13% of the country's energy use and 5% of its carbon footprint.

Meanwhile, in the developing world, many people face daily problems of access to clean water, not least in Africa and Asia—exacerbated by pollution from intensive farming, urbanization, and poor sanitation. More than 40% of the world's population experiences water stress, and almost 1 billion people in rural areas have no access to clean water. Consequently, as well as the obvious threats to human health and well-being, many freshwater species of wildlife are declining or facing extinction. Developed countries are also affected, with parts of the US, Spain, and Australia prone to water shortages.

Water scarcity is a regional, national, and international issue. Water is needed for manufacturing and energy production, where the end product may be used far from its source. Our global economy means developed countries rely on exports from developing countries, where water supplies are more likely to be under pressure.

Population growth

Medical advances and quality-of-life improvements mean that people are living longer than in the past, leading to population growth, especially in less-developed countries. The global population of 6.8 billion people is up from 6 billion in 1999 and projected to exceed 8 billion by 2025. Put simply, more humans mean more human activity, magnifying the environmental problems outlined above.

The global human population is growing steadily, putting more pressure on the Earth's resources.

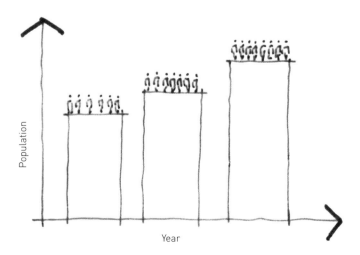

The construction industry

The construction industry has a massive ecological impact and the decisions designers make are major contributors to the environmental problems described above.

With respect to climate change, buildings account for up to 30% of global greenhouse gas emissions. They are the main source of carbon dioxide emissions in the developed world, producing almost half of world emissions. For example, buildings create 30% of the US's total greenhouse gas emissions and half of the UK's carbon emissions.

Much of this impact is attributed to the energy we use within buildings. Buildings are responsible for 40% of global energy use, more than any other industrial sector. Another significant factor is embodied energy in buildings, from the extraction, processing, and manufacture of new materials. In addition, greenhouse gas emissions are associated with transportation to deliver materials to and from site. Construction materials account for 30% of all road freight in the UK, where the manufacture and transportation of construction materials represent 10% of carbon emissions.

The built environment's impact on resources and biodiversity is equally harrowing. Buildings account for 20% of global materials use. Construction in Europe consumes more raw material by weight than any other industrial sector; in the UK, this translates as 350 million tons of material each year. In the US, buildings account for 30% of raw materials use. Construction's reliance on the logging industry is a major area of concern; in some countries, 80% of wood is sourced illegally, implying unmanaged habitat loss and contribution to climate change. With buildings using a quarter of the world's wood harvest, the construction industry has a responsibility to address the situation.

The construction industry also contributes greatly to waste, producing 20% of the UK's and 30% of the US's. This situation is not helped by a culture of over-ordering on building sites and a dearth of markets for recycled-content products.

As for our health, in the UK the Building Research Establishment has shown that volatile organic compounds (VOCs), released by paints, adhesives, and furnishings, cause headaches, eye and airway irritation, and tiredness. In addition, mold growth in interiors is known to trigger asthma and allergies. Conversely, better daylighting and natural ventilation in buildings result in people suffering from fewer headaches and less stress.

Buildings also contribute to potable water use, using as much as one-sixth of the world's clean water. In the US, buildings account for 12% of the country's clean water use.

Sustainability and the role of interior designers

"Insist on the rights of humanity and nature to coexist in a healthy, supportive, diverse, and sustainable condition."
WILLIAM MCDONOUGH (US ARCHITECT) AND
MICHAEL BRAUNGART (GERMAN CHEMIST)

Both for reasons of self-interest and a moral obligation to other species, we need to address these issues. We must act to safeguard our own survival and sanity by ensuring that humans always have access to food, energy, clean water, and the natural world. In parallel, we arguably have a duty to protect ecosystems and other species, since we have caused the problems, and we alone have the intelligence, communication skills, and knowledge to solve them.

The key to solving these problems is sustainability, or meeting today's needs without compromising those of the future. In the construction industry, this needs to be brought about through sustainable design, which applies this principle to all design decisions. While sustainability has social, economic, and environmental aspects, this book focuses on the environmental ones.

Given the construction industry's huge impact on the environment, designers can easily make a positive difference to environmental problems through their design choices, and indeed they have a responsibility to do this. Interior designers in particular can help, as they often work on renovation and residential projects, carefully select materials and finishes, and frequently choose lighting and appliances. Most interior designers are failing to embrace sustainable design, so progressive interior designers must take action to catch up with other designers in the construction industry. By 2013, around 50% of firms in the industry expect to be largely dedicated to sustainable building, so interior designers should be wary of getting left behind.

Interior designers are routinely involved in renovation, and are therefore ideally placed to address the

SUSTAINABILITY IS...

"...meeting the needs of today without compromising the ability of future generations to meet their needs."
United Nations World Commission on Environment and Development

built environment's biggest problem: its existing building stock. In the US and Canada, existing buildings account for 40% of carbon emissions, rising to 79% in New York. In the UK, existing buildings hold the greatest potential for reducing carbon emissions. And a study by the Athena Institute has found it is better to renovate existing buildings to improve their energy performance than to demolish and rebuild them. This makes sense, as even the most energy-efficient new building would take 20 years to cancel out the embodied energy expended in its construction.

Besides, renovation can make a real difference, creating an opportunity to upgrade a building's energy and water systems, and improve the thermal performance of its external envelope. New York's Empire State Building is being renovated to generate an energy saving of 38%, while renovating nineteenth-century homes could reduce their energy consumption by as much as 80%. More than 70% of current commercial and residential buildings are expected to still be standing in 2050, so sustainable renovation is vital.

"Sustainability is like teenage sex. Everybody says they're doing it, but very few people actually are doing it. Those that are doing it are doing it badly." ANONYMOUS, RELAYED BY ANDREW MAYNARD (AUSTRALIAN ARCHITECT)

Renovation projects, such as the Power House by Cannon Design in St. Louis (US), offer excellent opportunities to improve an existing building's environmental performance.

When needed, new-build offers a unique opportunity to create a sustainable fit-out with few limitations. It is reassuring that building sustainably can reduce emissions by 30 to 50% without a significant cost increase.

Frequent involvement in residential, and indeed hotel, projects means that interior designers can influence how we live. Simple design decisions such as including recycling bins, space to dry washing, and secure bicycle storage encourage occupants to follow a sustainable lifestyle.

Interior designers have the luxury of having plenty of time to choose materials and finishes for every element of an interior. Designers can use this time to consider the environmental impact of these materials; for example, by finding recycled-content materials, avoiding endangered tropical hardwoods, and limiting VOCs that harm human health.

Lastly, their role in choosing lighting and appliances means that interior designers can influence the energy efficiency and water consumption of buildings in use by selecting low-energy and water-saving products.

On new-build projects interior designers have the freedom to create a comprehensive sustainable project. Carr created both a sustainable envelope and interior for its modular Country Victoria House in Kilmore (Australia).

Above

Koby Cottage in Albion (US) by Garrison Architects enables its inhabitants to adopt a sustainable lifestyle, for instance by including bicycle storage.

Right

Interior designers are expected to invest a lot of time in choosing materials, often preparing sample boards like this one.

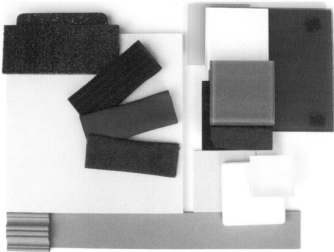

STEP BY STEP DESIGN IMPACT

It is important to recognize that every project has an impact on the environment during each stage of its life cycle, and that these impacts can be mitigated by sustainable design:

1 The interior designer creates a design.

2 The materials reach the site, having used energy and water, and caused pollution and waste during their manufacture.

3 The design is constructed, using more energy and water, and causing more pollution and waste.

4 The project is occupied. Running and maintenance require energy and water, and produce pollution and waste.

5 The interior is demolished, using energy, causing pollution, and producing waste materials.

History forgotten

Sustainable design is an inherent part of good design. In this section, we will look back through history to see many examples of good design, from traditional building types to twentieth-century Modernist design, that include sustainable features. Traditional building methods and Modernist designers often produced sustainable solutions, even if these were not driven by environmental motives.

Traditional buildings

Many examples of sustainable design can be seen in traditional, vernacular buildings from around the world. These typically used local, natural materials, simple construction methods, and local skills; were responsive to the site and climate; and exploited passive design principles. The buildings were sometimes portable, giving flexibility, and people's lifestyles were attuned to the local climate.

In passive design, the form, orientation, and internal layout of the building are used to derive free energy from the sun, daylight, wind, and building occupants. In hot climates, cool living spaces were often created at the base of tall spaces with high openings, which encouraged stack ventilation to remove warm air, while shutters and vines were used to provide shade from the sun. Conversely, in cold climates, living spaces were typically arranged around a hot core, such as a hearth. In both extremes, thick walls made of insulating materials were used to maintain a stable temperature inside. Rooms were sometimes arranged around courtyards, which would stay cool and shaded in summer but be warm and sheltered in winter.

Buildings were generally built in this way for practicality or out of necessity, using materials and skills that were readily available, construction methods that were easy to implement, and passive design methods that would assist survival. The result was sustainable, practical design with a simple beauty and regional character. While interior design was clearly not a primary concern, many of the principles are valid for interior design projects.

The igloo, Roman baths, Malay house, yurt, nomadic tents, and South Korean house are typical examples of traditional building typologies founded on passive design strategies.

The igloo is designed to exploit passive design for survival in the harsh Arctic climate. Its thick walls of compacted snow insulate the interior. Inside, an entrance lobby is formed to trap cold air, and living spaces are created on a raised shelf to take advantage of the warmer air toward the top of the space. Snow is clearly a natural material that is plentifully and locally available, while the simplicity of the igloo's construction means it can be built quickly by local people.

Roman baths combined passive design with energy efficiency, having an underfloor heating system. This heating method recycled excess heat from fire-heated basins feeding the baths. The waste heat was ducted beneath solid floors, taking advantage of their high thermal mass to disperse heat into the rooms.

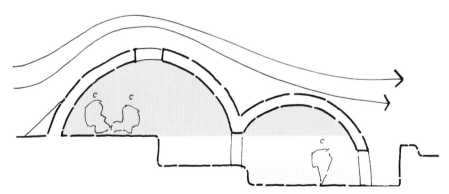

Above
This section through an igloo shows the thick walls protecting the interior from Arctic winds. The entrance lobby traps cooler air to prevent it reaching the inner living space. The living area occupies a raised shelf, benefiting from the warmer air toward the top of the space.

Right
Interior of an igloo showing the construction of compacted blocks of snow. This natural material is highly insulating, easy to build with, and locally abundant.

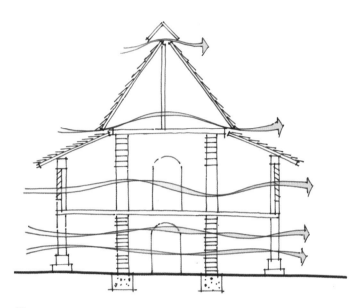

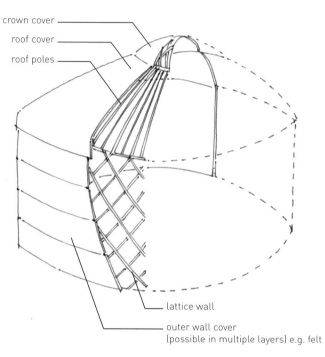

crown cover

roof cover

roof poles

lattice wall

outer wall cover
(possible in multiple layers) e.g. felt

Above
Section through a traditional
Malay house, which is designed
to remain cool in the hot,
humid climate.

Above right
Sectional diagram of a yurt
showing its simple construction
and ventilation outlet.

The interiors of traditional Malaysian houses are
cooled by natural cross-ventilation created by the door
and window locations, bringing relief from the hot,
humid climate. In addition, an opening at the top of the
roof encourages natural stack ventilation. The interior is
planned with a cool central core shaded by outer walls
and a deeply overhanging roof.

In contrast, the traditional South Korean home
uses passive design to keep its inhabitants warm. The
building is arranged around a sheltered courtyard, and
the external walls have high thermal mass for insulation.
Hot smoke from the kitchen is ducted under the floor to
heat the living rooms before being extracted through a
chimney. The floor construction of waxed paper over clay
on flagstones conducts the heat efficiently. The house
comprises natural materials, including a wooden frame,
clay floor, and clay or log walls.

The yurt (or ger) is used in many harsh environments,
from Mongolia to Siberia. It retains heat well, thanks to its
compact shape and insulating thick felt. An opening at the
top of the space provides ventilation to release smoke from
cooking and heating. Its simple pole-and-willow lattice
frame uses natural, locally available materials and can
be easily erected and dismantled. This brings flexibility,
allowing the occupants to move on when the
climate dictates.

Other nomadic tents are adaptable as well as portable.
Those of the Luri people in Iran have a goat-hair cover,
which keeps out the spring wind and rain, but is raised
in summer to admit cool breezes and provide shade.
The tents are moved from lower, warmer areas in winter
to higher, cooler areas in summer.

Modernist design

While the principles of these traditional examples are valuable, today's designers can perhaps better relate to more recent examples of sustainable design from designers practicing in the past few centuries. Many of the designers and design movements of this period incorporated sustainable measures. These included using local materials and skills; honestly expressing construction methods, materials, and function; responding to the climate; creating a link to nature; exploiting new technology; avoiding excess and waste; and building to last.

Again, concern for the environment was not the reason for these design decisions, which were made to follow a style or manifest the designer's philosophy on patriotism, humanity, technology, or humankind's place in nature. The outcome was stylish, well-designed buildings and interiors showing that appearance certainly need not be compromised by a sustainable approach. We continue to revere many of these designers as icons and pioneers of modern design. And their work, which typically aimed to create a total work of art covering the building, interior decoration, and furniture, is highly relevant to interior designers. Notable examples are Sir Edwin Lutyens, Charles Rennie Mackintosh, Frank Lloyd Wright, Walter Gropius, Alvar Aalto, and Charles and Ray Eames.

Lutyens English Arts and Crafts designers, such as Sir Edwin Lutyens (1869–1944), were inspired by the traditional, vernacular approach to construction described above. Reacting against industrialization, they advocated a return to craftsmanship and using indigenous materials. Lutyens used different natural materials to suit what was traditionally available near the site: tiles and wooden frames in Surrey; flint and red brick in Norfolk; local stone in Northumberland; and white-painted wood in Kent. As with the traditional buildings they followed, Arts and Crafts designs were built to last, reducing the need to consume resources for future repair and replacement.

Mackintosh Scottish architect and interior designer Charles Rennie Mackintosh (1868–1928) was identified with the Art Nouveau movement, which took nature as the inspiration for its decoration. Mackintosh's interiors, not least the Willow Tea Rooms (1903–4) in Glasgow (UK), show an abstract interpretation of plants, such as roses, buds, stalks, and, of course, willow trees. This symbolism pervades all elements of the interior of the tearooms, including the furniture, light fixtures, carpets, signage, and stained glass. Simply depicting nature is perhaps a superficial approach to sustainable design. Yet, crucially, it serves to remind us of our connection with the natural world and its value to us, even when we are farthest from it: indoors and in an urban environment. Besides, Mackintosh went further with the Willow Tea Rooms. The project renovated an existing building, avoiding wasteful rebuilding. He used mainly natural materials, such as oak paneling, silk and velvet upholstery, and wooden furniture. The interior shows an economy of design, getting the most out of components to avoid waste. The dominant, high-backed chairs double as space dividers, thereby serving two functions with minimal materials. Mirrors are used to reflect natural light around the spaces, getting the most out of the daylight from the windows and roof lights.

Charles Rennie Mackintosh's Willow Tea Rooms in Glasgow (UK) were inspired by natural forms, reminding visitors of the value of nature. The decoration on the chairs and lighting is an abstract representation of plants. The tall chair backs help divide the space, using materials economically by serving a dual purpose.

"[The artist] must possess technical invention…and above all he requires the aid of invention in order to transform the elements with which nature supplies him—and compose new images from them."
CHARLES RENNIE MACKINTOSH

Wright Architect Frank Lloyd Wright (1867–1959) encapsulated the approach of the American Prairie School, which built on the ideas of the Arts and Crafts movement, and employed traditional local materials while benefiting from new technology. Wright designed many interior elements for his buildings, believing that furnishings and lighting should be an integral part of the design. His own house and studio in Oak Park (1893) in Chicago (US) uses local, natural materials such as wood shingle and paneling. These are expressed in an honest way, whereas new materials are exploited for structural elements but are not celebrated. Wright uses stained glass to admit filtered natural daylight. The interior spaces are arranged in an open plan around a central hearth, warming the heart of the building. This organic approach to planning is based on natural forms, underlining the significance of nature. His traditional building methods and materials were durable and built to last.

Gropius Designer Walter Gropius (1883–1969) founded the influential Bauhaus school of art, design, and architecture in 1919. Bauhaus designers combined all the arts and crafts, and embraced new technologies, using mass production and new materials. Their preference for factory prefabrication, sparsely furnished interiors, and restrained, demountable plywood furniture made efficient use of materials and limited waste during the manufacturing process. They pioneered scientifically assessing environmental performance, calculating daylight, sunlight, and heat loss in their designs. Gropius's interior of the director's office at the school's original base in Dessau in Germany (1923) shows the functional, machine-age elegance that typifies the Bauhaus style. The furniture is simple to allow for mass production; the light fixtures were modeled on industrial versions; and the floorboards and walls are exposed except for a rug and tapestry designed by Bauhaus students. This reveals an economy of design that avoids waste or excess.

Aalto The Scandinavian style, which Finnish architect Alvar Aalto (1898–1976) represented, saw a return to celebrating natural, local materials, particularly wood, and responding to regional climate. Aalto enhanced traditional building methods with new technologies. He explored the relationship between humankind and nature through his work, seeking to create a harmony between the two. Aalto derived his forms and order from nature, and sought to blur the boundary between the interior and exterior. Moreover, he filled his interiors with natural daylight and sunlight. Like Wright's, Aalto's designs were robustly built, minimizing the need for maintenance.

Aalto's design for Säynätsalo Town Hall (1949–1952) is no exception. The spaces are planned around a raised courtyard, giving shelter and shade. A corridor around the perimeter of the courtyard mediates between inside and out. Its plentiful natural light, exposed brick walls and floors, and plants give the impression of being an outdoor space. Natural materials, comprising wood, stone, clay brick, and copper, are used throughout. They give the interior a tactile quality, through features such as leather-bound door handles, exposed brick walls and floors, and wooden screens. Man-made materials

The Bauhaus director's office in Dessau (Germany) by Walter Gropius exhibits a functional elegance that exploited the latest technologies of its era. Prefabricated components, bare walls, and sparse furnishings avoid any wasteful use of materials.

"Any building for humane purposes should be an elemental, sympathetic feature of the ground, complementary to its nature environment."
FRANK LLOYD WRIGHT

are also used and exposed—for instance, polished screed floors and painted concrete ceilings—avoiding excessive finishes. Similarly, mass-produced pendant lights show an openness to using new technology alongside traditional construction. And processed natural materials, like the locally made birch plywood wall paneling, exploit the best of both worlds by using a natural material efficiently.

Eames American designers Charles and Ray Eames (1907–1978 and 1912–1988) evolved the Bauhaus approach, using mass-produced materials in a simple way. Their prefabricated Eames House (1949) in Los Angeles (US), with its off-the-shelf components, is a case in point. The interior is filled with daylight, sunlight, and plants, which lend it an uplifting atmosphere. It includes many examples of the couple's own furniture designs, such as a leather and bent-rosewood easy chair, which use natural materials in a simple, machine-made way.

"Who ever said that pleasure wasn't functional?"
CHARLES EAMES

Loos and Mies van der Rohe Interior designers can also learn from the philosophy of two other practitioners from this period: Adolf Loos, whose mantra was "form follows function," and Ludwig Mies van der Rohe, who coined the phrase "less is more." Although both men were driven by a minimalist aesthetic, these statements can equally be applied to sustainable design. They underline the importance of using resources sparingly and efficiently, rather than being wasteful by creating an over-complicated design.

We have seen that there is much to gain from revisiting the work of past designers and the methods used in traditional construction. Yet the world has changed considerably over the last century, resulting in many of the design principles from the past being forgotten. Our economies are global, not local; developing countries offer cheap production and are understandably intent on catching up with Western lifestyles. Western society is extremely image-conscious, creating a culture of continual design makeovers, in which retail and hotel branding is continually refreshed, and we renovate our homes and move on. Our increasing wealth has turned us into insatiable consumers who no longer "make do and mend," fueling a throwaway society. Our lifestyles are dependent on technology and energy, and as we can largely control the internal climate, we no longer work with the external climate. Most worryingly, we have arguably become disconnected from the natural world, and have lost our sense of humankind's place in and duty toward nature. Lastly, we are healthier and living longer, so population growth is compounding our impact on the Earth. None of these trends is sustainable and it is time we revived some of the design methods of the past.

The corridor of Alvar Aalto's Säynätsalo Town Hall in Finland feels like an outdoor space. Daylight, exposed brick walls, plants, and views of the courtyard constantly remind visitors of their place in nature.

"[Design] cannot disengage itself from natural and human factors…. Its function rather is to bring nature ever closer to us."
ALVAR AALTO

Relearning

Climate change and other environmental issues are problems that need solving urgently. Luckily, designers are by definition problem-solvers, and are in an ideal position to provide solutions.

It is paramount that emerging interior designers take responsibility for the situation and help effect change through their work by reconsidering how they design. As the established mainstream of the interior design profession is not responding adequately, it falls to developing designers to set standards for the future. Many of these will be younger people, who have grown up with a high awareness of environmental issues, and will be most affected by the mounting consequences of climate change.

This book is aimed particularly at emerging designers, to help them incorporate sustainable thinking into everyday design practice. Sustainable design should not be, and we cannot afford to let it be, an optional extra. It is an essential part of good design and should be ingrained in good design practice. Sustainable design is relevant to all building sectors and project programs— and can be affordable on all budgets.

Eventually legislation, peer pressure, and the market will force designers to consider sustainability. Many countries are setting themselves ambitious targets to reduce their carbon emissions, and the construction industry offers easy carbon cuts for governments. Making the cuts will be a quicker, more comfortable, and more effective process if designers take the lead.

The UK has some of the most ambitious targets in world, with the government pledging to reduce emissions by 80% from 1990 levels by 2050. All new housing in the country will be zero carbon by 2016, with public and other nondomestic buildings expected to follow suit by 2018 and 2019, respectively. This will be enforced largely through building regulation updates. Other countries' aims for reducing greenhouse gas emissions by 2050 include 80% for the US and 50% for New Zealand from 1990 levels; and 60% for Australia and 75% for France from 2000 levels.

Other countries, particularly in Western Europe and Scandinavia, are already world leaders. Sweden currently has the toughest building regulations in terms of fabric and energy performance requirements. The stringent Passivhaus environmental standard for housing is widespread in Austria and Switzerland, and mandatory in Sweden and parts of Germany.

The challenge need not be taxing. We can reflect on approaches that have worked well in the past and reuse those that are still valid. We have already seen that there are many lessons to be relearned from historic architecture and interior design, from the vernacular through to twentieth-century Modernism.

Relearning knowledge and habits from history will allow interior designers to take responsibility for and help address the unique issues of our time. By revisiting past approaches such as passive design, use of local

Target reduction in carbon emissions by 2050 (%) (from 1990 levels)

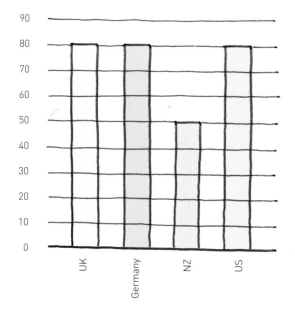

Target reduction in carbon emissions by 2050 (%) (from 2000 levels)

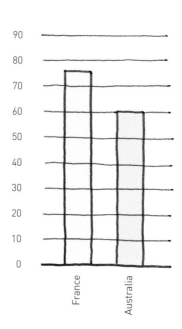

Far left
Graph showing carbon-reduction targets from 1990 levels for key countries. (Sources: NHBC Zero Carbon Compendium, The *Guardian*, UK Department of Energy and Climate Change.)

Left
Graph showing carbon-reduction targets from 2000 levels for key countries. (Sources: NHBC Zero Carbon Compendium, The *Guardian*, UK Department of Energy and Climate Change.)

materials and skills, built-in flexibility, honest expression of materials and construction, and prefabrication, we can combat environmental problems on a practical level. Further, by reviving ideals such as reinforcing our connection with nature and promoting a lifestyle that is in tune with the natural world, we can approach the issues at a fundamental, philosophical level. Although the approaches were not developed with sustainability in mind, but simply good design, they can be revived to serve this purpose.

Of course, we should not lose sight of what we have learned in recent decades. For maximum impact, designers can enhance past principles with new materials, technologies, and knowledge. The ultimate aim is to design sensitively and appropriately, creating projects that have a minimal environmental impact and so "tread lightly" on our planet. With this approach, we can address the key environmental issues explored in the opening section—of climate change, diminishing resources and biodiversity, waste, allergies and stress, and water scarcity.

Designers can influence climate change by reducing carbon emissions through their choices of energy system or supplier, products, and materials. Using renewable energy, energy-efficient products, and low-embodied energy materials can all make a tangible difference.

The choice of materials also has a significant effect on resource and biodiversity depletion. Specifying renewable materials, such as fast-growing bamboo and wood from well-managed forests, will help ensure that the Earth's resources are replenished and that habitat loss is reduced.

Waste can be reduced by retaining usable elements from an existing space, using prefabricated components, and sourcing reclaimed or recycled materials. Meanwhile, avoiding virgin plastics prevents waste that remains in landfill sites for millennia.

Interior designers can even affect the health of people using their interiors. Avoiding chemicals, for example in paints and fabrics, and including plants, daylight, and natural ventilation promotes well-being.

Finally, interior designers can address water scarcity by choosing water-saving appliances, or considering rainwater harvesting and graywater recycling.

Interior designers have nothing to lose and plenty to gain from embracing sustainable design. As well as dealing with critical problems, it will bring about a return to quality, thoughtfulness, and consideration in design.

Today's interior designers can take advantage of the latest technology to produce a sustainable design. Here, prototype light-emitting wallpaper by Jonas Samson uses high-tech illuminated sheets to make a product that efficiently performs both a decorative and a practical function.

Disregarding preconceptions

Some designers who set out to be sustainable develop extreme opposition to modern processes, materials, and styles, relying solely on traditional sustainable solutions. Using only conventional environmentally sound materials and construction techniques, such as wooden frames, straw bales, and earth walls, can give designs a very specific look. Although such projects are undoubtedly sustainable and worthwhile, restricting the design solution for all projects in this way is unnecessary and would lead to a prescriptive "eco" style where all sustainable designs looked similar.

While a rustic eco style can be appreciated for its traditional and natural qualities, it does not appeal to everyone, making it a niche product. Some undoubtedly see it as old-fashioned and regressive, perhaps having negative associations with hardline environmentalists in wooly sweaters and sandals. Understandably, this image can put off interior designers and clients who are keen to make their projects "greener" but seek a modern appearance.

Although it is important to recognize the practical value of traditional materials and construction, this need not dictate the appearance of a project nor limit sustainable design to one particular style. As shown in an earlier section, there is undoubtedly much to learn from the past, but the potential of modern technology should not be disregarded. Traditional, natural materials can be used in a slick, modern way or combined with newer materials for a more balanced palette.

Nevertheless, there is nothing wrong with your design looking "green" if that is your intention. Some designers deliberately cultivate an eco style, wanting to make a

In his own house at Takoma Park near Washington, D.C. (US), Bill Hutchins of Helicon Works has created a beautiful example of eco style. Its salvaged wood components and straw-bale walls coated in natural plaster have been deliberately expressed to make a feature of their irregular, organic forms.

statement and highlight their environmental credentials, and there are many successful designs that demonstrate this beautifully. But it is important to understand that this is just one of many approaches to sustainable design.

   The only approach that should always be avoided is "greenwash" (see also page 90), when a green gimmick is used to imply that a design is more sustainable than it really is. This could range from adding a token wind turbine to a project that contributes little to its energy needs, to instaling wood laminate flooring that has a surface veneer from a renewable source on a non-renewable wooden backing.

   It is essential to acknowledge the opportunity designers have to be both sustainable and contemporary. By incorporating both traditional and modern approaches intelligently, it is possible to create attractive and original designs that do not scream "eco style," but instead look like any other good design.

   In fact, a truly sustainable approach means considering the whole life cycle of a project, optimizing its functionality and quality, and therefore the experience of its users. A successful project addresses all critical design issues: far from isolating sustainability as an optional extra or afterthought, sustainability lies at its core. Therefore, environmentally conscious design that also takes account of other project needs is inherently good design.

   Throughout the book, we shall discover a wide range of ways to design more sustainably while achieving a contemporary style.

Hill House in Merricks (Australia) by Mihaly Slocombe Architects, demonstrates that a traditional sustainable building technique can become a beautiful feature within a modern, sophisticated interior. A rammed-earth wall, formed from the site's clay soil, creates a focal "spine" along which the living spaces are arranged and provides thermal mass to help regulate the internal air temperature.

Above
Drawerment by Jaroslav Jurica of Hubero Kororo Design Group uses a mixture of drawers salvaged from office furniture.

Right
Jurica has installed the drawers within new casements built into the wall to give them new life, achieving a successful integration of old and new.

Why this book is required

Interior designers need guidance to embrace the challenge of creating sustainable designs. Unfortunately, most information on sustainable design, in books and on websites, focuses on architecture. Similarly, the legislation that governments have brought in to combat climate change primarily targets architects. Even assessment tools have typically been developed with whole buildings in mind. Although many of these resources are applicable to interior designers in part, there is a need for information to suit their specific interests and needs.

The task of incorporating sustainability into interior design is at least as difficult as incorporating it into architecture. First, interior designers tend to work within existing buildings more frequently than architects, or within a shell created by an architect. This places restrictions on what can be done that do not exist when starting anew—and it eliminates many opportunities to control energy use through passive design. With a new building, architects have the luxury of making fundamental decisions about the site layout, building form, and envelope to ensure the spaces are well insulated and make best use of natural solar heat, daylight, and ventilation. They can also design in efficient energy and water systems from the outset.

Second, interiors are frequently intended to be short-lived, whereas buildings are usually intended to last many years. The project duration influences the decisions a sustainable designer makes, partly determining whether a particular material or construction method is a sustainable choice. Architects can routinely take a long-term view on which construction methods, energy and water systems, and materials are appropriate to minimize environmental impact throughout the life of the design.

But interior designers must take greater account of how long their designs will be in place and what will happen to the materials afterward.

There is no reason for interior design to be overlooked. As we have seen earlier, interior design plays a significant role in the construction industry's vast impact on environmental problems. The energy-inefficient existing buildings that interior designers often work within represent the biggest threat to climate change in the built environment. The high rate of change in interior design, with interiors being regularly refreshed and remodeled, means the profession generates a significant quantity of waste. And the exotic materials that interior designers are sometimes tempted to specify can be associated with high embodied energy and the depletion of rare resources.

Without proper support or regulation, too few interior designers are taking the initiative to incorporate sustainable thinking into their projects. This book will provide interior-specific guidance, highlight the resources that already exist for interior designers, and show inspiring examples of pioneering interior projects that manifest sustainable design.

We have seen in this chapter that environmental issues are reaching crisis point, and the construction industry, including interior design, is partly to blame. But, given proper guidance, there is potential for interior designers to deploy their problem-solving skills, combining past principles with modern technology, to find solutions through their work. And all this can be done without compromising the appearance of their designs.

CHAPTER 2 A SUSTAINABLE APPROACH

32   INTRODUCTION

32   EMBRACING COMPROMISE

36   CONSIDERING CONSEQUENCES

38   ASKING THE RIGHT QUESTIONS

53   ASSESSMENT

Introduction

We have learned in Chapter 1 that sustainable interior design is essential to help address global environmental problems. In this chapter, we will explore how to approach designing interiors with a low environmental impact. We will explain the need for compromise and to consider the consequences of one's design decisions, and introduce a series of questions that structure this process. Further, we will outline the assessment tools designers can opt for to formalize their approach to sustainable design.

Embracing compromise

First we will cover the often-inevitable need for compromise. Sustainable design involves considering many issues and making complex choices, so there is not always one obvious, perfect solution. In addition, other design constraints may dictate which sustainable measures are feasible, and other members of the design team may have responsibility for areas of the design that have the highest environmental impact. Interior designers must accept these limitations and embrace the challenge of doing the best they can. This section offers advice on overcoming some of the common barriers to a sustainable design approach.

The unsustainable nature of construction

It is a common reaction to feel daunted by the unsustainable nature of construction, the enormity of the world's environmental problems, and the contradictions and limitations inherent in sustainable design.

Sadly, all building activity is environmentally damaging to some degree, and no building method or material is completely benign. Whether its purpose is immensely beneficial to society or a more frivolous creative exploration, any interior design project uses up natural resources, energy, and water, and creates pollution and waste during its construction and use. Thus it is impossible to practice interior design without causing any environmental damage.

It is tempting to be defeatist and conclude that the only way to be truly sustainable is to stop designing altogether and make do with what we already have. But this will never be a viable solution in our society, so rather than give up we must find ways to temper the impact of our lifestyle.

"Nothing is unthinkable, nothing impossible to the balanced person, provided it arises out of the needs of life and is dedicated to life's further developments." LEWIS MUMFORD, US WRITER

The scale of the problem

Scale is the next potential barrier, as global environmental problems are huge and an individual project is a small part of the cause. Furthermore, an interior designer's role on the project can seem small, with many key aspects of the design, such as the façade and energy system, often outside of their control. In the same way that a homeowner might doubt the global impact of installing a low-energy lightbulb, an interior designer might doubt the value of choosing one material over another, when design decisions with greater environmental consequences are beyond their scope.

Faced with this reality, interior designers can appreciate the need to design with more consideration for the environment, yet may not be convinced they are able to make a significant impact. It is easy to feel powerless, taking the attitude that if it is not possible to make a palpable difference, it is not worth trying at all. Nevertheless, even small measures can be effective, particularly when repeated across many projects and by many designers. Moreover, given the huge environmental impact of the construction industry as a whole, every consultant is vital in influencing a shift toward a more sustainable approach.

"We all moan and groan about the loss of the quality of life through the destruction of our ecology, and yet each one of us, in our own little comfortable ways, contributes daily to that destruction." ED ASNER, US ACTOR

Knowing where to begin

Even once an interior designer has committed to developing more sustainable solutions, it can seem hard to know where to begin. Environmental issues are extremely complex, so it is easy to feel overwhelmed. Any given building material will have redeeming features as well as negative environmental impacts. On the one hand, bamboo is a renewable natural resource; on the other hand, it has high embodied energy once transported outside Asia, and some sources may deplete panda habitat.

Rather than be discouraged, the interior designer must weigh up the pros and cons of every product to decide whether the positives outweigh the negatives. In some instances, this will be an objective decision; in others, it will depend on the designer's opinion of which environmental issues should be given the highest priority. Armed with an understanding of the environmental issues to look out for, designers can begin to make informed comparisons. It is worth both questioning materials that are assumed to be sustainable and reconsidering those that are sometimes dismissed as unsustainable.

Bamboo epitomizes the fact that many materials can be seen as both good and bad in terms of their impact on the environment.

Approaching compromise

In an ideal world, a designer would conceive and develop the best possible solution to a project brief and given space, experiencing a smooth transition from drawing board to site. Unfortunately, this is an unrealistic scenario, as many external influences will prevent such a perfect process. By the same token, other design restrictions—such as cost, working within an existing envelope, and resistance from the design team—can conflict with sustainable design. The smart designer will be aware of these influences and accept that compromises need to be made along the way.

Sustainable design can be more expensive, but this is not always the case. A choice between two materials that have quite different environmental impacts could make no difference to the cost. Sustainable design can even save money, either in the short term, by omitting unnecessary components, or in the long term, by reducing energy bills or maintenance needs. Some renewable energy systems, such as photovoltaic panels and low-energy lightbulbs, do have a relatively high capital cost, but the investment is ultimately recouped through reduced running costs. Besides, grants are often available to help with the initial investment. Similarly, using natural paints usually has a cost premium, but the resulting improvement in air quality can bring savings through improved productivity and reduced absences among staff. Clients may want to invest more in order to have a sustainable design, either for its own sake, to improve occupant well-being, or to achieve environmental accreditation for their interior.

It is common for interior designers to work within an existing building. This often rules out any scope to control fundamental elements to assist in a sustainable

Investing in natural paints helps to ensure good indoor air quality.

outcome, especially if the building has heritage value that prevents significant modification of the interior. This could be viewed as a restrictive disadvantage for interior designers, enforcing compromise from the outset. But it is important to recognize that the very nature of inheriting an existing building or space means reusing something old or obsolete, rather than throwing it away and starting anew. Many interior design projects are therefore already taking a basic sustainable approach at their outset, preventing buildings going to waste and saving on the need for new materials. Interior designers have a great opportunity, and indeed duty, to upgrade and breathe new life into these spaces. There may be elements that are restrictive and others that are beneficial, but the best approach is to look at what exists, make good use of it, and improve it.

On many projects, an interior designer will work within a large project team. As well as the client, end user, and contractor, the interior designer may work alongside a range of consultants and organizations, including architects, engineers, estimators, project managers, local authorities, historical commissions, and suppliers. These diverse groups sometimes have conflicting agendas, and may not see sustainability as a high priority among other project considerations. It is important to be prepared for this and anticipate their potential objections to sustainable design choices, such as the cost of installing LED lighting or planning constraints on erecting wind turbines. The best approach is to focus on what you can do within these parameters, and to be willing to convince other people of the merits of an environmentally sound design choice where it really matters. As well as advocating the environmental strengths of the proposal, it is a good idea to highlight other advantages—such as durability, ease of construction, or rating system credits—that will have a broader appeal. Few people set out to harm the environment, so the team is likely to support sustainable design, providing it simultaneously addresses other concerns.

It is clear that, given all the above constraints, a totally environmentally inert project is an unachievable ideal. It is therefore crucial to accept that everything we do will have some impact on the environment and compromise will often be essential. Yet designers have a responsibility to begin to tackle these problems rather than continue to add to them, using their skills to improve the situation.

Although it is rarely possible to create a design that is entirely sustainable, it is always possible to choose the best of the available options to create spaces that are less damaging to build and more efficient in use than the norm. We can assess the adverse impacts of every product against the benefits it would bring, and compare it with similar alternatives. This method should be repeated for every choice throughout the design process. With this approach, an interior designer can make decisions that will each make a difference, minimizing the overall environmental impact of the design.

To be effective, this process must be underpinned by in-depth knowledge of the environmental implications of using a particular material, system, or process. Once we fully understand the consequences of our choices, we can have confidence in our judgment as to how best to proceed.

The skillful interior designer will try to preempt constraints that may be outside their control, and to influence other members of the project team to incorporate sustainable measures within their scope. They will address environmental considerations with optimism and as best they can, as a core challenge in creating an inspirational design solution. Interior designers are well placed to embrace this challenge, as they are accustomed to compromising when renovating existing buildings or fitting out a given shell. Sustainable thinking can simply become an integral part of their usual design approach, forming a routine consideration in good design practice.

"You can't save the world, but you can set it an example."
ALVAR AALTO, FINNISH ARCHITECT AND DESIGNER

At Malmaison Oxford Castle in Oxford (UK), Jestico + Whiles transformed a former prison into a quirky boutique hotel. The original gallery has been retained as a dramatic foyer, and several prison cells are joined together to create each luxurious bedroom.

Considering consequences

We have already noted that, in order to make informed choices, or compromises, the interior designer must fully appreciate the consequences of every design decision. We will now discuss how these consequences can be considered by understanding the life cycle of a project.

Much of a project's impact on the environment occurs after it has been completed, when the interior designer is no longer involved. After the certificate of occupancy has been issued, operating and maintaining the space will continue its contribution to environmental problems, as will its eventual demolition. Energy and water will be used to run the building; potent chemicals may be used for cleaning and redecorating; new materials will be needed for repairing and replacing components; and significant waste will be produced when the interior becomes outdated or redundant. But all these aspects can be controlled by decisions made during the design process. Hence, it is paramount for designers to understand the life cycle of a project, and take responsibility for the consequences of their designs.

The life cycle begins with demolishing any existing building or interior to make way for the project, and continues after the design period, through the operation phase, to what happens after the new interior's demolition. A sustainable life cycle forms a genuine circle, with the demolished materials being reused or recycled to make new products for another interior. Unfortunately, many projects have a more linear life cycle, with much of the demolished material becoming landfill waste. The sustainable version was coined "cradle to cradle," after the book of that title by William McDonough and Michael Braungart, while the unsustainable, linear version is known as "cradle to grave." Cradle to cradle takes the principle that the natural world achieves equilibrium because there is no waste, and much of the environmental damage caused by human processes could be avoided by finding ways to eliminate waste.

Needless to say, there are environmental impacts throughout a project's life cycle that need to be considered. So the interior designer must both evaluate the effects of producing the interior—by understanding each product's journey from its raw materials to its installation—and think beyond this, considering how the space will be used and maintained, and what will happen at the end of its life.

This comprehensive approach should be built into all stages of the design process. It is all too easy to be

There is no waste in the natural world, which operates in balanced, continuous cycles. Deciduous trees shed their leaves once they no longer nourish the tree; the fallen leaves decay on the forest floor and release nutrients into the soil to encourage the growth of the tree and its seeds.

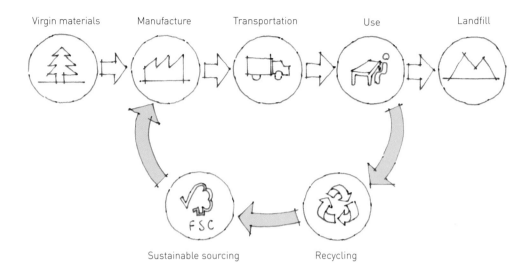

Virgin materials Manufacture Transportation Use Landfill

Sustainable sourcing Recycling

FSC

A sustainable life cycle forms a closed loop, with all by-products being reused. An unsustainable life cycle is a linear model, with waste as its outcome.

"To eliminate the concept of waste means to design things—products, packaging, and systems— from the very beginning on the understanding that waste does not exist." WILLIAM MCDONOUGH (US ARCHITECT) AND MICHAEL BRAUNGART (GERMAN CHEMIST)

distracted by more immediate pressures, such as time, budget, and the demands of the project team.

At the outset of a project, an interior designer's focus is often led by the client's fundamental requirements: the functions the space needs to accommodate, and the desired aesthetic style, delivery time, and budget. When time and budget are limited, designers may be inclined to select familiar, cheap materials and products, hastily thrown together to create a quick and easy fit-out. Even with adequate time and money, the desire to create a striking design can produce an extravagant and inappropriate solution, for the sake of image and reputation. In either case, once the project is completed, it is easy for a designer to feel their work is done and move on to the next project without considering what will become of their creation once handed over to the user.

In our fast-moving culture, where people expect instant gratification, this is a common reality that designers must resist—not least because such a short-sighted approach is unlikely to result in a high-quality design solution. While the successful delivery of the project is undoubtedly important, a good design will also address longer-term issues to ensure the space works well, provides healthy conditions for its occupants, and has a minimal ongoing impact on the environment.

One outcome of a short-sighted design approach might be occupant discomfort. If, to save time and money, the interior designer has used materials that release fumes after installation or located occupied spaces away from natural light and ventilation, the interior could have poor air quality. This may affect the well-being and productivity of the occupants and, in a workplace, increase staff absences. In the long run, not planning ahead to take account of the whole life of the design wastes time and money if the design fails and has to be remedied.

To avoid this happening, consideration of the full life cycle should be incorporated into the design process. This can be done informally, with reference to guidance, or formally, through life-cycle assessment.

Crucially, an interior designer must learn to ask the right questions at the start of a project, scrutinize the purpose of a design, and make informed choices about energy and water systems, materials, and construction methods that acknowledge the whole life cycle of the design. Looking at each stage of the life cycle helps the designer to see the bigger picture, recognize the long-term environmental impacts, and be empowered to make more sustainable design decisions.

A wealth of informal guidance is available to help designers expand their knowledge of sustainable design and make informed choices based on a life-cycle approach. Knowing your priorities is fundamental and simple mantras, such as "reduce, re-use, recycle," can help define these. This is elaborated on in Chapter 3, which sets out basic priorities for choosing energy and water systems, materials, and construction methods. The same chapter highlights useful material specification guidelines that assist with making product choices on a much more detailed level.

More in-depth methods of assessing your design have been developed via the use of evaluation tools known as Life Cycle Assessments or Analyses (LCAs). These assess the design as a whole to arrive at a certified rating, as described later in this chapter. Isolated components of the design, such as a product, can also be formally assessed and will be covered in Chapter 3.

Asking the right questions

To create a successful sustainable interior, the designer needs to ask themselves the right questions throughout the design process and assess all the consequences of their decisions over the project's life cycle. The following seven questions form a prompt to help interior designers work through the design process and ensure that all stages of the life cycle have been considered with a view to developing a sustainable design. These questions should be worked through as soon as the designer embarks on the project, to inform the conceptual design decisions while there is still time to make a difference. They should then constantly be referred to as the design develops and more detailed decisions are made. Finally, reflecting on them when the project is complete and occupied can be a valuable learning tool to benefit subsequent projects.

Sustainability is just one aspect of a design and should not constrain other critical project aims. The questions help the interior designer to ensure that sustainability is not only thoroughly considered, but incorporated appropriately, with due regard to project-specific factors.

The questions can be used as an alternative to, or in support of, more sophisticated life-cycle assessment methods. They are generic and can therefore be applied to any type of project. They are designed to draw out how the specific nature of a project, especially its intended longevity, will set the approach to sustainable design. The questions begin to identify and group together project types according to the length of time they are expected to last, be they temporary, flexible, or long-term.

The questions begin with fundamentals and become more detailed, so many of the answers to the initial questions will inform the responses to the later questions. The order corresponds to both the progression through a project's life cycle and the sequence in which the questions are likely to become relevant.

What is the purpose of the project?

↓

How long will the interior be required?

↓

What energy and water systems are appropriate?

↓

What materials are appropriate?

↓

What construction methods are appropriate?

↓

How will the space function?

↓

What will happen to it when it is no longer useful?

1. What is the purpose of the project?

This question is so fundamental that it could easily be overlooked. However, it is critical to deciding which sustainable measures will be appropriate. From the outset, it is essential to fully understand what the client and the brief are asking you to produce to ensure that the project is relevant and worthwhile. Each project brief will demand different solutions from a designer and therefore there is no one standard approach.

The purpose means what the nature of the project is, what activities will happen in the space, what kind of people will use it, when it will be used, and what ambience it should create. These considerations must underpin the interior designer's selection of energy and water systems, materials, and construction methods.

The nature of the project could be a fit-out of a new-build project or a renovation of an existing space— each of which comes with its own opportunities for and constraints on sustainable design. A renovation will preclude many passive design strategies, but will allow

In this renovation of a fashion boutique in Athens (Greece), dARCH Studio reused furniture from the existing store, giving it new life by attaching it to the walls to form quirky display shelving.

Top
This sketch for The Box Project by NoChintz explores the idea of the space being used as an exhibition stand at the 100% Design exhibition, London (UK).

Above
Here the potential of using The Box Project as a retail unit is explored.

Opposite
Clive Sall Architecture and Carl Turner Architects's sketch for the Design Council offices in London (UK) shows how the "train" element will accommodate different functions.

materials to be salvaged from the demolition stage and reincorporated in creative new ways.

The interior could be used as a school, home, office, restaurant, movie theater, hotel, nightclub, or anything else. It may even be required to accommodate multiple uses. Whatever the use, it will have specific technical requirements—in terms of acoustics, fire safety, accessibility, health and safety, and maintenance—that must inform all aspects of the design and may limit the choice of systems and products.

The interior may be intended for children, adults, groups, staff, or the public. The complexity, zoning, and heights of the controls for the energy and water systems should reflect the expected demography. Children could be encouraged to use less energy with low-level light switches and fun energy-use displays. Office workers are more likely to be swayed by convenience, therefore lighting and heating controls should be near exits, and zoned to coincide with different areas or groups. Members of the public are unlikely to take responsibility for switching off lights, so automatic controls would be worthwhile.

The space could be occupied continuously, during the day, by night, or only for short periods. The energy and water systems, and their controls, need to take this into account. Materials should be chosen to withstand the wear and tear from the expected pattern of use.

The ambience sought for an interior can vary greatly. Should the feel of the spaces be slick or traditional, light-colored or dark, fun or conservative? Should sustainability be expressed or covert? Such decisions are central to the look of the design and will dictate what kind of materials and construction methods the interior designer should consider.

This question should be posed when embarking on a new project and referred back to throughout the project to test the developing design. The interior designer must first understand the aims of the project, through site analysis, research, absorbing the program, and through dialog with the client. During this process, both the opportunities and constraints associated with sustainable measures can be assessed. The interior designer can then plan realistic outcomes for the design that aspire to a sustainable solution.

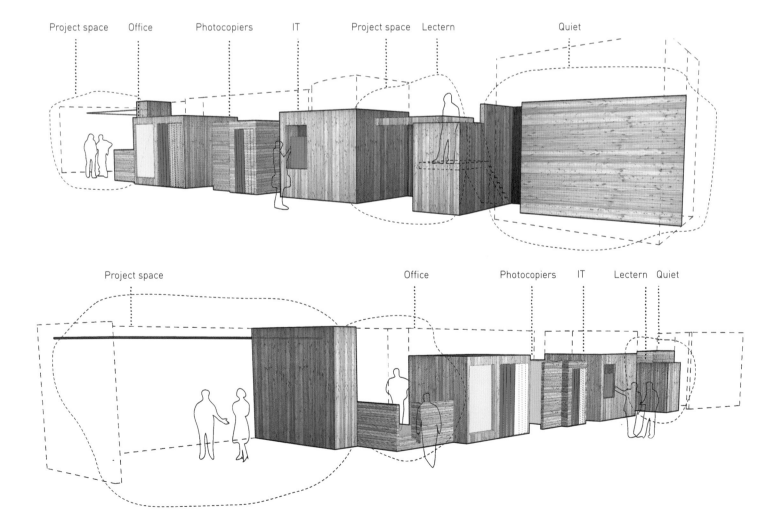

2. How long will the interior be required?

The second question is less obvious, but the answer often unlocks the most appropriate approach to sustainable design. Knowing how long the completed interior is likely to remain in place empowers designers to choose energy and water systems, materials, and building techniques that are suited to this time period. In addition, it allows the interior designer to plan accordingly for demolition, flexibility, or future adaptability.

It is not necessary to know exactly how many weeks, months, or years the interior will last, simply whether it will be temporary, flexible, or long-term in nature. These three categories each have quite different requirements and implications. The options for an exhibition project provide a good illustration of the varied requirements. An exhibition could just be for a one-off show, required for perhaps one week and then never used again, and therefore a temporary project. Alternatively, it might be required to travel around the world, being repeatedly installed and dismantled for months or even years, and having inherent flexibility to adapt to different spaces. Conversely, it might be a permanent, static exhibition in a museum that would not need to change in the foreseeable future and must be built to last a long time. A different

design approach is demanded for each of these scenarios to ensure a successful and sustainable project.

It is evident from the above example that the three project categories are not necessarily dictated by building type, so it is worth defining them before we go further.

Temporary projects are short-term with a very limited lifespan. The end date will often be known when the project commences and will be no more than one or two years from the certificate of occupancy date. Such projects require a "light touch" to their design, using materials, construction methods, and energy and water systems that have a minimal environmental impact. It is not worth investing in a complex, expensive, hard-wearing, or high-energy solution that will be required for only a short period. Temporary projects provide a great opportunity for designers to develop simple and clever solutions from sparse materials.

A flexible project is one that needs to accommodate changes in layout or use, either being flexible enough to accommodate daily changes or adaptable to adjust to longer-term changes. It will commonly be a medium-term project, such as a retail unit leased for, say, five years. However, a flexible project might equally be temporary

Left
Temporary projects, such as Artek's exhibition at the Milan Furniture Fair (Italy), allow designers to use materials sparingly and inventively. Artek's chairs were stacked to provide the wall decoration at the same time as being exhibited.

Opposite
This sketch for the Howies store in Bristol (UK) by Remodel indicates how freestanding display furniture will be used on the store floor to allow flexibility to change the layout.

or long-term. Whatever the case, its flexible nature overrides its duration as the main influence on the approach taken to sustainable design, so flexible projects are treated as a separate category. The retail unit example would be designed to represent the company brand and effectively sell its products, but would also need to accommodate changes in fashion and stock from season to season. The interior might therefore form a constant backdrop to an evolving product-display system. Flexible projects call for interior designers to be ingenious, innovative, and forward-thinking in order to create adaptable and practical spaces.

Many interior projects are intended to last indefinitely; as no project is truly permanent, these are classed as long-term. In this instance, the priority is to invest in long-lasting, durable materials and integral energy and water efficiency, while taking into account ongoing operation, cleaning, and redecoration. One good example of a long-term project is a home. Long-term projects demand a far-sighted approach from their designers, who should try to allow for future advancements, such as new materials and technologies, to be added and should respond to predicted challenges, like the effects of climate change.

Again, this is a question to ask at the beginning of every project, as the answer should set the designer's approach to sustainable design and influence many choices throughout the design process. The answer should initially be sought from the client or program. However, if the client is uncertain how long the finished interior will remain in place, the interior designer must make a judgment based on their experience of similar building types. Once the duration and requirements for flexibility are known, the interior designer can tune their approach to sustainable design accordingly.

In Chapter 3 we will investigate in more detail how choices of energy and water systems, materials, and construction techniques differ for the three project categories. Chapter 4 then groups exemplar projects into these categories to review their different approaches to sustainable design.

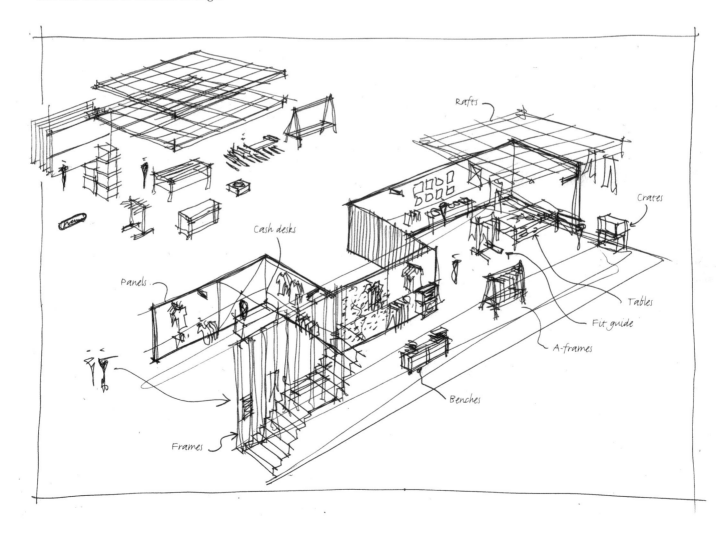

3. What energy and water systems are appropriate?

This question asks how energy and water should be provided to and distributed around the interior. The answer will depend on the answers to questions 1 and 2, as well as on the project's location. As we will see in Chapter 3, the purpose of the design and its expected duration affect which passive strategies and renewable technologies, for both energy and water, are feasible and relevant. For instance, underfloor heating would be more appropriate in a space that functions as a school, occupied continuously throughout the day, than a house whose occupants are out all day. This is because underfloor heating works at low temperatures, gradually heating up a space, and cannot provide short bursts of high heat. On temporary projects, passive design and energy efficiency will be the main focus, whereas long-term projects may also look to renewable energy generation.

It is also important to establish the local climatic conditions, the amount of energy and water needed to run the space, the hours of use, and the budget. All these factors should influence the choice of system, as we will see in Chapter 3.

This question should be tackled as soon as initial ideas about energy and water provision are entertained, and revisited whenever related products, such as faucets, are being selected. The interior designer must establish the determining factors outlined above through site analysis, studying the program, and discussion with the project team. They can then draw out the viable options for the energy and water system and identify the most sustainable solution that works for the project.

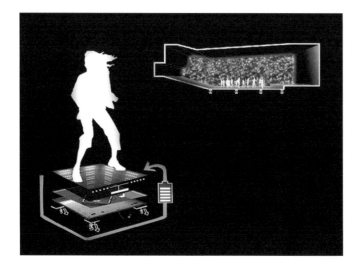

Above
This three-dimensional drawing for Club Watt in Rotterdam (Netherlands) by Studio Roosegaarde develops the concept of using the movement of dancers to power lights within the dance floor. The movement of each dancer is converted into electricity that powers colored LED lights within the top layer of the floor structure.

Below
Ripple Design's section through the Courtyard House in Los Angeles (US) illustrates how passive design will be exploited to provide free energy for heating and ventilation. Thick walls, floors, and ceilings provide thermal mass, soaking up heat from the sun to warm the interior. The sloping ceiling draws warm, stale air out of a high-level roof light.

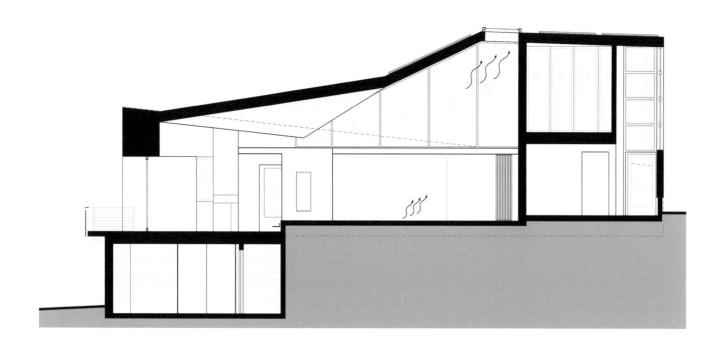

4. What materials are appropriate?

The interior designer must carefully consider which materials and finishes to use to realize their designs. The materials could be natural or synthetic, virgin or recycled, simple or high-tech, local or exotic.

Again, the answer to this question will be closely linked to the responses to questions 1 and 2. The interior's purpose and longevity should inform the approach to embodied energy and water, durability, air quality, and waste associated with its materials. Avoiding materials that impair air quality may be a major concern in a building where children spend a lot of time, such as a crèche. In temporary projects, it is perhaps more important to source materials that can be reused or recycled once the interior is dismantled.

In parallel, designers must consider the site location, budget, construction schedule, cleaning and maintenance strategy, aesthetic qualities, and technical performance when seeking a sustainable material.

Along with generating the overall concept for a project, building up a palette of materials for the design is one of the first things an interior designer will do in the design process. Fortunately, deliberating over materials is well within an interior designer's comfort zone, so sustainability is merely an extra dimension to assess. They should already consider the color, texture, light reflectance, density, weight, flexibility, smell, durability, and performance of potential materials. To make environmentally conscious choices, characteristics such as embodied energy, recycled content, renewability, and air quality must be added to this list.

Bligh Voller Nield's sketch of the reception of the Green Building Council Australia's headquarters in Sydney explores use of color, materials, and plants to create a welcoming environment.

Remodel demonstrates how existing materials, such as glazed brick walls and wooden rafters, will be exposed in the Howies store in Bristol (UK) in this visualization.

With their thorough knowledge of materials, interior designers are in an ideal position to ensure that materials are used efficiently and in a way that harnesses their natural qualities. There is a vast range of materials available for use within interiors, all with different attributes. The innate qualities of a given material will lend themselves best to certain applications. Using the most appropriate material for the situation in the most efficient manner is a sustainable approach, as it avoids the need for compensatory products or finishes. For example, using materials with reflective or light-colored surfaces in a dim space might reduce the need for electric lighting. Using virgin wood as a thin veneer over recycled wood board limits the impact on deforestation. Likewise, toxic finishes can be avoided by using exposed brick walls instead of painted gypsum wall board.

"An honest use of materials, never making the material seem that which it is not, is a good method. Materials... must be used optimally, never using one material where another can do the job less expensively, more effectively, or both." VICTOR PAPANEK, AUSTRIAN DESIGNER AND EDUCATOR

Clearly, this question should be posed every time the interior designer chooses a material or finish. Once the project-specific factors affecting material choices have been established, the available materials should be understood through research, discussion with manufacturers, obtaining samples, and viewing examples of the product in use. The interior designer then has the means to arrive at a solution that is sustainable, fit for purpose, and beautiful.

5. What construction methods are appropriate?

How the materials are put together on site is just as important as the materials themselves. The construction methods could be traditional or modern, quick or slow, wet or dry, and expressed or disguised.

The most suitable construction techniques will be informed by the interior's purpose and anticipated longevity. In an education building, it might be desirable for the construction methods to be made visible, with obvious connectors, to act as a learning tool. In an occupied building, it will be important that the construction limits disruption and avoids toxic processes to protect the occupants. In a temporary project, it is sensible for materials to be attached in a way that facilitates disassembly, and avoids bonding different materials together, to allow for recycling. Lightweight, movable, or folding elements may be essential for a flexible project, whereas long-term projects require construction methods that are solid and robust.

Cardboard has inherent strength from its corrugated hollow core, making it an efficient material. This was one reason why it was chosen by Molo for its Softwall screens.

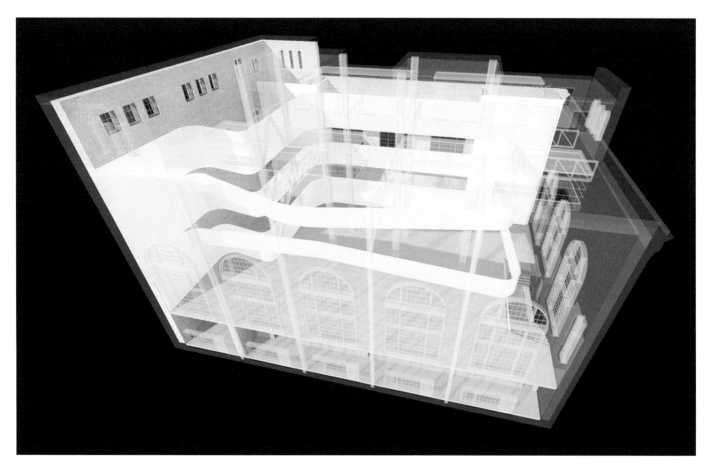

This drawing of the Power House in St. Louis (US) shows Cannon Design's idea of constructing a new structure within the shell of the existing building.

Other key influences include the site location, budget, construction schedule, performance requirements, and demolition strategy. The site location determines which manufacturing processes and labor skills are available in the vicinity. The budget may mean that certain high-technology building systems are unaffordable. A high-pressure construction schedule for a retail unit that must open in time for Christmas shopping is unlikely to allow for laborious, traditional construction methods: a prefabricated solution that is quick to install might be the best option.

This question should be answered in tandem with question 4, as the construction methods must suit the proposed materials. All materials have physical strengths and weaknesses that lend themselves to particular installation methods. Throughout the design process, the choice of materials and construction methods will continually inform one another, and should be combined to make the most of a material's inherent qualities. The interior designer should review the project-specific requirements through site surveys, analysis of the program, and team meetings. They will then be in a position to consider the viable construction options, before choosing which will be best for the project and the environment.

6. How will the space function?

A successful design stems from an understanding of how the finished project will be used by people. Considering this question helps interior designers ensure that their designs represent the best possible solution for the end users, as well as the most sustainable one. Designers should understand how the end users will occupy the interior; how they will operate the energy and water systems; how the space will be cleaned and maintained; how recycling will be managed; and how their design will affect well-being. These factors will help determine whether a flexible design solution is appropriate, and how the design can promote sustainable behavior and health in its occupants.

Flexible spaces are sustainable because they make maximum use of available space and allow the interior to be altered rather than replaced when its occupants' needs change. We discussed flexible spaces under question 2, but it is worth dwelling here on whether flexibility will enhance how the occupants use the interior. It is also important to highlight that any project can include flexible elements, whether or not it is meant to be flexible as a whole. Could a space or piece of furniture be used for more than one purpose? A meeting room could double as a place for staff to eat lunch; circulation areas could also be used for exhibitions; and seating benches could contain storage.

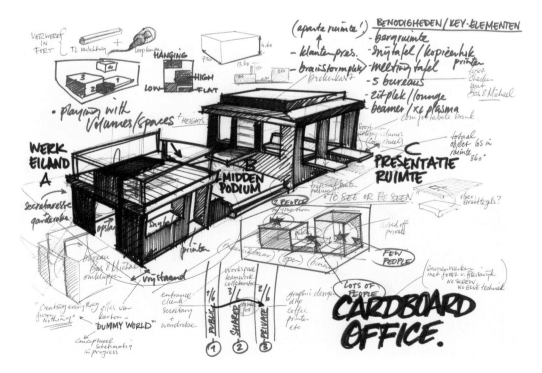

This early sketch for Alrik Koudenburg and Joost van Bleiswijk's Nothing office in Amsterdam (Netherlands) suggests how different areas of the design might be used.

Basic design decisions can encourage or deter sustainable behavior. Conserving energy and water, recycling, and cycling can either be made effortless or inconvenient by the design. The interior designer can plan spaces and furniture to make best use of natural light, discouraging occupants from turning on artificial lighting. In a library or office this might mean putting study spaces near windows, and circulation and storage toward the darker center of the interior. Having separate switches for lighting over areas receiving less natural light supports this principle. Similarly, heating and ventilation should be easy to control in individual areas. Simple measures such as providing a clothesline in a garden or over the bath in a ventilated bathroom mean that homeowners need not use a dryer. Understanding how recycling will be separated and collected, and providing sufficient recycling bins near the source of the waste, will help the system run smoothly. For example, a photocopying area should include space for a recycling bin. Composting can also be allowed for in buildings with outdoor space or access to food-waste collections. Providing showers and secure bicycle racks in an office will encourage staff to cycle to work.

As well as functioning effectively for its occupants, an interior ought to help them feel healthy and happy. The temperature should be comfortable, the spaces well lit and ventilated, and the air clean. The interior designer can help by exploiting natural light and ventilation, avoiding materials and finishes that impair air quality, and including indoor plants that filter pollutants.

This question should be answered when developing the initial design concept and reconsidered throughout the design process. The interior designer should ascertain how the space will be used by interpreting the program,

Below left
Compartmented recycling bins are a space-saving way of encouraging people to recycle their waste.

Below right
House plants can be used in an interior to enhance air quality.

initiating a dialog with the end user, studying similar interiors in use, and, if possible, observing how the occupants currently operate. It is helpful to document your intentions for how the space should be used, in the form of a simple manual that can be given to the end users. This could include furniture layouts; recycling procedures; strategies for cleaning and maintenance; instructions for controlling heating, ventilation, and lighting; expected annual energy and water use; and material safety data sheets. It is valuable to go further, visiting the interior and obtaining feedback from its occupants once it has been in use for a while to see whether the space is being used as intended.

TIP USER MANUAL

Preparing a simple, brief user manual on the interior for the occupier will help them use the space to its optimum efficiency.

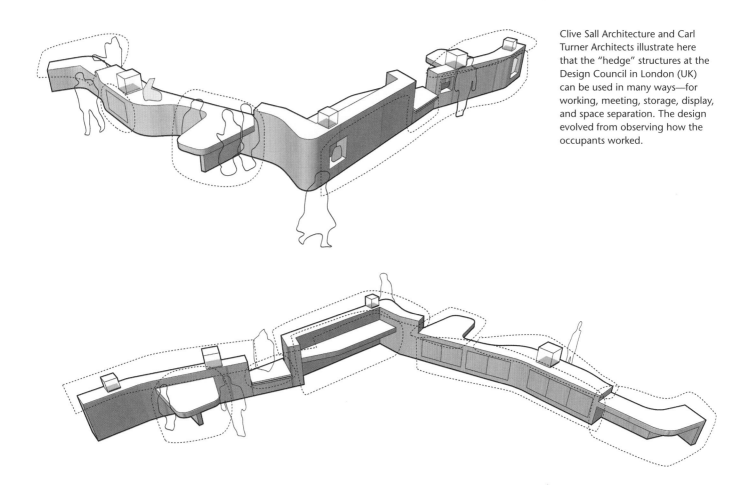

Clive Sall Architecture and Carl Turner Architects illustrate here that the "hedge" structures at the Design Council in London (UK) can be used in many ways—for working, meeting, storage, display, and space separation. The design evolved from observing how the occupants worked.

7. What will happen to it when it is no longer useful?

This final question can seem so remote from the design stage of a project that it is all too often forgotten. But a project's destiny at the end of its life has a profound effect on waste and, consequently, use of new resources. This is true for projects of any duration: failing to consider the end of a temporary project is frankly inexcusable, but it is also crucial to recognize that even a long-term project will eventually be replaced.

The interior designer must preempt the end of the interior's life at the beginning of the design process, choosing materials that can readily be reused or recycled and installation methods that support this. If it is unavoidable that materials will end up in landfill, biodegradable natural materials are usually a better choice than enduring synthetic materials such as plastics. In long-term projects, construction methods should aid separation of even nonrecyclable materials, in case technologies and markets become available for recycling them by the end of the project's life. Ensuring that the design limits dust and fumes during demolition is also worthwhile, as, for example, medium-density fiberboard (MDF) releases harmful wood dust and formaldehyde when disturbed.

This question should be considered when specifying materials and construction methods. The interior designer should consider whether the materials can be reclaimed or recycled once no longer needed, and whether the construction methods enable this.

Nevertheless, the project's duration will affect the approach to demolition. It should be possible with temporary projects to either reuse or recycle most elements of the design, aiming for a quick demolition process and easy removal that leaves the site as it was found. Flexible projects will often be capable of adapting to suit a new function, but the interior designer should allow for furniture, fixtures, and equipment that might no longer be needed to be reclaimed or recycled. The interior designer should aim for these items to be removed with minimal damage to the shell, to allow the next tenant to use the original background. The underlying electrics and plumbing should be planned to accommodate a change in layout or function, perhaps being distributed through circulation areas behind removable floor and ceiling panels. By thinking ahead in this way, the interior designer can reduce unnecessary waste and new materials when their project is replaced. With long-term projects, it is much harder to predict what will happen at the end of the interior's life, but using recyclable materials is the best approach.

Skylab Architecture's drawing for the North Office in Portland (US) shows new modules inserted within the existing building that can be removed intact for reuse or recycling.

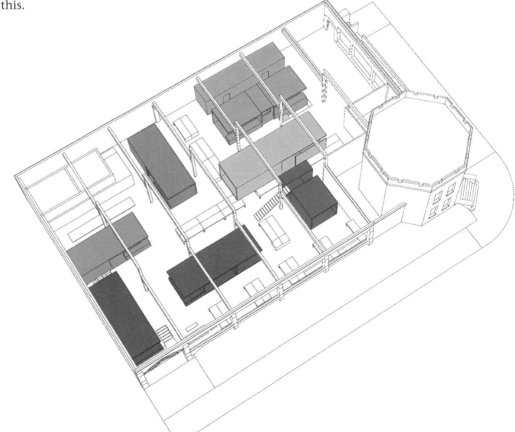

Assessment

Assessment and certification systems offer a way for designers to formalize a sustainable approach to design. The whole design is assessed, using calculation and measurement, to give a scientific, objective evaluation of its likely environmental impact. This is worthwhile, both for designers to check that their good intentions are resulting in sustainable design, and to demonstrate this to clients and occupants. Achieving certification on a project can be an excellent marketing tool for designers and a valuable selling point for clients.

Whether or not an interior project is being formally assessed, many of the certification systems' websites offer excellent guidance and informal assessment tools, which can help the interior designer develop a design that has minimal environmental impact. Although the specifics of the systems are usually tuned for use in particular countries or regions, the online tools can be consulted as a useful guide for a project in any part of the world, as the principles of sustainable design are universal.

Many assessment systems are aimed at the whole building and focus on new-build projects, so are most suited to interior designers working alongside an architect. However, increasingly they extend to renovation and fit-out projects, making them more relevant for solely interior projects.

Certain whole-design assessment systems, such as LEED, BREEAM, and Green Star, allow designers themselves to become accredited professionals, reflecting their knowledge and experience of sustainable design.

Less comprehensive systems exist that assess a particular aspect of a design; for example, a material or appliance. These are discussed in the following chapter, under energy, water, or materials, as appropriate.

Whole-design assessment systems are typically carried out during the design stage, but sometimes include some post-completion checking. An independent, accredited assessor carries out the assessment using a standard checklist. Projects score points against criteria under key environmental topics; the topics are generally weighted to reflect their relative environmental impact, energy usually being ranked highest. The total number of points scored corresponds to a rating, grading the design's environmental performance from standard to high.

Designers liaise with the assessor to provide design information to underpin the assessment and to agree which points to target. They must then ensure that they follow what was agreed throughout the design process and can show evidence of this. The assessor will allow a margin of comfort in case unforeseen issues prevent targeted credits being gained. The certification bodies publish useful guidance documents to help designers understand the system and how to achieve a high-scoring design.

Assessment systems are typically voluntary, but might be required by some clients, particularly public bodies. They usually involve a fee, although some free online tools exist. Most certification bodies have a series of standard assessments geared at particular building types and locations. These can be adapted by the assessor to suit most situations to encompass new, existing, whole-building, and interior-only projects. In addition, a number of interior- and renovation-specific standard assessments have emerged, and this trend looks likely to continue as the certification systems develop. Most assessments focus on environmental sustainability, but some also cover social and economic issues.

In this section we will outline the main whole-design assessment systems that are available worldwide, explaining the sectors they cover, their scope, categories, ratings, and at what stage they apply. The principal systems are LEED, BREEAM, Ska Rating, NABERS, Green Star, Green Globes, BEAM, CASBEE, and DGNB. Of these, LEED and BREEAM are perhaps the best known and most widely used. However, some of the more specialist systems are of particular relevance to interior designers, such as Ska Rating, which is intended for interior fit-outs, and NABERS, which measures the performance of existing buildings.

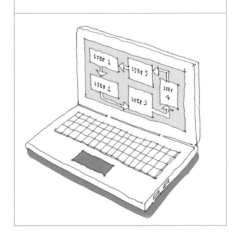

TIP ONLINE TOOLS

Use tools and guidance freely available on most assessment websites to carry out an informal assessment of your project.

Case study LEED assessment

The Power House, St. Louis (US) by Cannon Design

Cannon Design obtained a LEED Gold rating for its own office, The Power House. The renovation successfully addressed all the assessment categories.

The interior is a conversion of a former steam-generation plant in downtown St. Louis in the US, scoring highly for regeneration and public transportation connections under Sustainable Sites. The provision of cycle storage and showers was also rewarded in this category. Points were awarded under Energy and Atmosphere for upgrading the existing windows with low-emissivity insulated glass and avoiding CFC-based insulation. Water Efficiency measures include harvesting rainwater to irrigate plants and using efficient sanitary fixtures.

High levels of natural daylight and the specification of carpets, paints, adhesives, and sealants with low Volatile Organic Compound (VOC) content ensure good indoor air quality. Elsewhere, materials and resources have been conserved by reusing most of the existing building fabric, recycling site waste, choosing products with recycled content, and providing storage for recyclable waste.

Measures like a sustainable operations plan for staff, a commitment to using green cleaning products, and exceeding LEED standards by sourcing 40% of building materials locally were recognized as innovative.

The thermal performance of the existing windows has been enhanced using insulated glass with a low-emissivity coating.

Left
An operations plan ensures that the office is run in a sustainable manner.

Below left
As seen in the café, the existing walls, floors, and ceilings have been reused to conserve materials and resources.

Below right
Working areas, such as this meeting room, benefit from high levels of daylight. Low-VOC carpets and paints promote good indoor air quality.

LEED

Leadership in Energy and Environmental Design (LEED) is run by the U.S. Green Building Council. While applicable globally, it is especially prevalent in North America. The system covers a wide range of building types, including commercial interiors, schools, retail, healthcare, and homes for both new construction and existing buildings. The assessment covers all stages, from design to construction to operation.

The assessment categories are: Sustainable Sites, Water Efficiency, Energy and Atmosphere, Materials and Resources, Indoor Environmental Quality, Innovation and Design Process, and Regional Priority. The LEED for Homes Assessment has two further categories: Locations and Linkages, and Education and Awareness. The categories are weighted, with the energy category given the highest value. There are four ratings: Certified, Silver, Gold, and Platinum.

Designers can become LEED Green Associates or, at a more advanced level, LEED-accredited professionals (LEED-APs).

LINK **www.usgbc.org/leed**

LEED India

India's version of LEED, LEED India, is run by the Indian Green Building Council for new buildings and major renovations in the office, retail, education, and hotel sectors. The assessment is made during the design and construction stages, using the same categories and ratings as LEED itself. Again, a professional qualification can be gained under the system.

LINK **www.igbc.in**

BREEAM

Based in the UK, the Building Research Establishment's Environmental Assessment Method (BREEAM)—along with the affiliated EcoHomes and Code for Sustainable Homes—is used worldwide, particularly in the UK, Europe, and the Gulf. Like LEED, these systems cover most sectors, spanning offices, retail, education, industrial, residential, justice, healthcare, and international. A bespoke assessment is also available for anything outside of these standard categories. Both new and existing buildings can be assessed; there are standard assessments for existing healthcare facilities and buildings in use, while one for domestic renovation will soon be available. BREEAM applies during the design, post-construction, and operation stages.

Again, energy is ranked highest among the categories, which consist of Energy, Transport, Pollution, Materials and Waste, Water, Land Use and Ecology, Health and Wellbeing, and Management. BREEAM has five levels: Pass, Good, Very Good, Excellent, and Outstanding. The Code for Sustainable Homes, for assessing new homes, is rated from 1 to 6, with 6 being the best; BREEAM EcoHomes, which is used for existing housing, gives a single score as a benchmark for homeowners to improve upon.

BREEAM offers a BREEAM-AP accreditation for design professionals.

LINK **www.breeam.org**

Ska Rating

Unlike most assessments, Ska Rating has been developed for interior projects only. The building shell is not taken into account and therefore does not affect the score. Every aspect of the interior is considered, down to coat hooks and adhesives. Ska Rating is run by the Royal Institute of Chartered Surveyors (RICS) in the UK and is for office fit-outs. It is a relatively new initiative and its scope is expected to expand, with retail fit-outs being the next planned project type.

Assessments are carried out at the design stage, at handover (i.e. when the certificate of occupancy has been issued), and one year after occupation. The post-occupation assessment does not influence the score

but provides useful feedback on whether key design intentions for energy consumption, water use, and recycling have been achieved. The full assessments can be done informally by the designer using the free online tools or, to get a formal certificate, by an independent assessor. The web-based assessment includes useful guidance on how to measure best practice.

Assessment categories are Energy and Carbon, Waste, Water, Materials, Pollution, Wellbeing, Transport, and Other. Each category contains a series of good-practice measures, which are optional, so that the project is scored only against those measures that are applicable. There are four ratings: Unclassified, Bronze, Silver, and Gold.

LINK **www.ska-rating.com**

NABERS

The National Australian Building Environmental Rating Scheme (NABERS) is primarily for existing buildings, covering offices, homes, hotels, and shopping malls. NABERS rates energy, water, waste, and indoor environment performance based on measured data, such as energy and water bills. The system therefore offers a focused, highly relevant assessment for interior designers specializing in renovation projects.

Projects are assessed during occupation, using performance data for the previous 12 months, and are awarded a star rating of up to 5 stars. An assessment could be carried out before and one year after renovation to measure any improvement brought about by the design.

LINK **www.nabers.com.au**

Green Star Australia

Both new-build and renovation projects in Australia can be assessed under the Green Building Council Australia's Green Star system. Its scope includes residential, healthcare, retail, industrial, education, and office projects, with a specialist assessment for office interiors. A new system for existing offices is in the pilot stage.

Scoring results in a rating from 4 to 6 stars and is based on nine categories: Management, Indoor Environment Quality, Energy, Transport, Water, Materials, Land Use and Ecology, Emissions, and Innovation. These categories are weighted differently depending on the project's location within Australia: for example, water is weighted higher in southern than northern Australia, as availability of drinking water is a more significant issue in the south of the country.

The Green Star Australia Accredited Professional qualification allows designers to demonstrate their experience of the system.

LINK **www.gbca.org.au**

Green Star New Zealand

The New Zealand Green Building Council has its own version of the Green Star assessment system, adapted for the specific context of New Zealand. Its nine weighted categories are the same as Green Star Australia's and again produce a rating from 4 to 6 stars. Standard assessments are available for offices, office interiors, and industrial and education buildings.

Similarly to the Australian version, a Green Star New Zealand Accredited Professional qualification is available.

LINK **www.nzgbc.org.nz**

Green Globes

Green Globes is the Green Building Initiative's assessment system for North America. New and existing commercial buildings achieve a rating from 1 to 4 globes based on their performance under the criteria of Energy, Indoor Environment, Site, Water, Resources, Emissions, and Project/Environmental Management.

LINK **www.thegbi.org**

BEAM

The Building Environmental Assessment Method (BEAM) is used in Hong Kong and China for all building types, and both new and existing buildings. A system for interior fit-outs is currently being developed. Run by the BEAM Society, the system considers Site Aspects, Materials Aspects, Energy Use, Water Use, Indoor Environmental Quality, and Innovations and Additions. These categories are weighted, with energy given the most importance. The assessment leads to a rating of Bronze, Silver, Gold, or Platinum, and is conducted following completion of a project.

LINK **www.beamsociety.org.hk**

CASBEE

Japan GreenBuild Council's Comprehensive Assessment Systems for Building Environmental Efficiency (CASBEE) has weighted categories for Energy Efficiency, Resource Efficiency, Local Environment, and Indoor Environment, producing a rating from 1 to 5. A CASBEE assessment is carried out during the design and occupation stages. It is used throughout Japan and Asia, and suits homes and renovation projects. There is also a tailored assessment for temporary projects.

LINK **www.ibec.or.jp/CASBEE**

DGNB

The German Sustainable Building Council's DGNB assessment has three scoring levels: Bronze, Silver, and Gold. Its categories consist of Ecological Quality, Economical Quality, Social Quality, Technical Quality, Quality of the Process, and Quality of the Location, and are weighted differently depending on the building type being assessed.

DGNB is carried out during the design and construction phases. It focuses on new buildings in the office, retail, industrial, education, and residential sectors, as well as existing offices.

LINK **www.dgnb.de**

Assessments that are specific to interior projects, like Ska Rating and some of the standard assessments becoming available under other assessment systems, are a welcome and much-needed development. This will hopefully continue to spread across all the assessment systems as they develop, giving interior designers worldwide the means to formally evaluate the environmental merits of their designs for all building types.

This chapter has shown that interior designers must be prepared to compromise and rigorously consider the consequences of their design decisions when approaching sustainable design. We have seen that working through a series of questions throughout the design process is a sensible method of ensuring that all environmental issues are considered over the project's whole life cycle. Further, this process can be usefully supported by the many assessment tools that are available to check a project's environmental impact.

Case study Green Star assessment

Green Building Council Australia headquarters, Sydney (Australia) by BVN

The Green Building Council Australia's (GBCA's) headquarters in Sydney, achieved a 5-star Green Star Australia rating. Bligh Voller Nield's (BVN's) design was assessed under the Office Interiors system. The client sought an interior that would demonstrate sustainable construction and provide a healthy, pleasant working environment.

The fit-out scored points under all nine Green Star categories. Management points were gained for producing a tenant guide and waste-management plan to monitor the percentage of waste that is recycled. Lease clauses requiring monitoring against energy-, water-, and waste-reduction targets, as well as the use of green cleaning products, address land use and ecology. The building's city-center location ensured easy points for proximity to public transportation and limiting the number of parking spaces. Innovation was rewarded for using indoor plants throughout the office and incorporating a wormery for composting kitchen waste.

An efficient displacement ventilation system and lighting on motion sensors contribute to significant energy savings in comparison with similar offices. Water use is minimized through dual-flush toilets, water-saving faucets, and waterless urinals, as well as a graywater system that filters wastewater from washbasins, the kitchen sink, and dishwasher for flushing the toilets. Unnecessary finishes have been avoided by leaving building systems and concrete floors and ceilings exposed. Low-impact materials include salvaged chairs, low-VOC carpet tiles, recycled-plastic tack boards, and tables made from low-formaldehyde board. Non-ozone-depleting thermal insulation also tackles greenhouse gas emissions. The plants, including a living wall behind the reception, promote good indoor air quality, while excellent daylight provision and views further support employee well-being.

Above left
A living wall of climbing plants screens the workspace from the reception and enhances air quality.

Above
The office benefits from daylight, panoramic views, and indoor plants to promote staff well-being. Ceilings, floors, and building systems are exposed where possible to limit finishing materials.

Left
The lounge area in front of reception includes second-hand furniture. This creates a welcoming, cozy atmosphere and avoids the embodied energy associated with manufacturing new furnishings.

STEP BY STEP ASSESSMENT PROCESS

BroadwayMalyan's office fit-out of Auckland House in Swindon (UK) achieved a Gold Ska Rating. Qualified Ska assessor, Hurley Palmer Flatt, carried out the assessment online, following the process set out below:

1 After registering with the website, basic project details, such as the project name and address, floor area, and personnel, are entered on this page.

2 The target rating is chosen, in this case Gold, by deciding how many of the potential sustainable design measures can be achieved. This page shows that 55 measures were targeted.

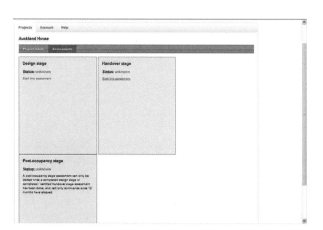

3 A design stage assessment is started at an early stage in the design process. This page allows you to choose whether to work on the design stage, handover (certificate of occupancy) stage, or post-completion assessment.

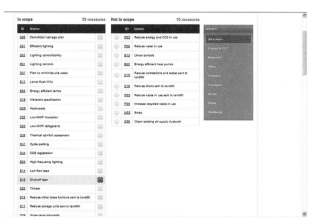

4 Scoping is carried out to select which criteria are applicable to the project under the eight assessment categories of Energy and Carbon, Waste, Water, Materials, Pollution, Wellbeing, Transport, and Other. Here Efficient Lighting and Hardwoods have been included, and Bricks have been excluded, from the project scope.

5 The design stage assessment is carried out during the design process. The interior designer or assessor decides whether the design meets each criterion and lists evidence of compliance. Online guidance is provided to assist with this. The assessment is completed at the end of the design process, giving a predicted rating. Auckland House achieved 51 of its targeted 55 measures, maintaining a Gold rating, which requires a minimum of 50 measures.

6 The assessment is repeated at the certificate of occupancy stage to check that the predicted rating has been achieved.

7 Finally, a post-completion assessment is undertaken one year after certificate of occupancy.

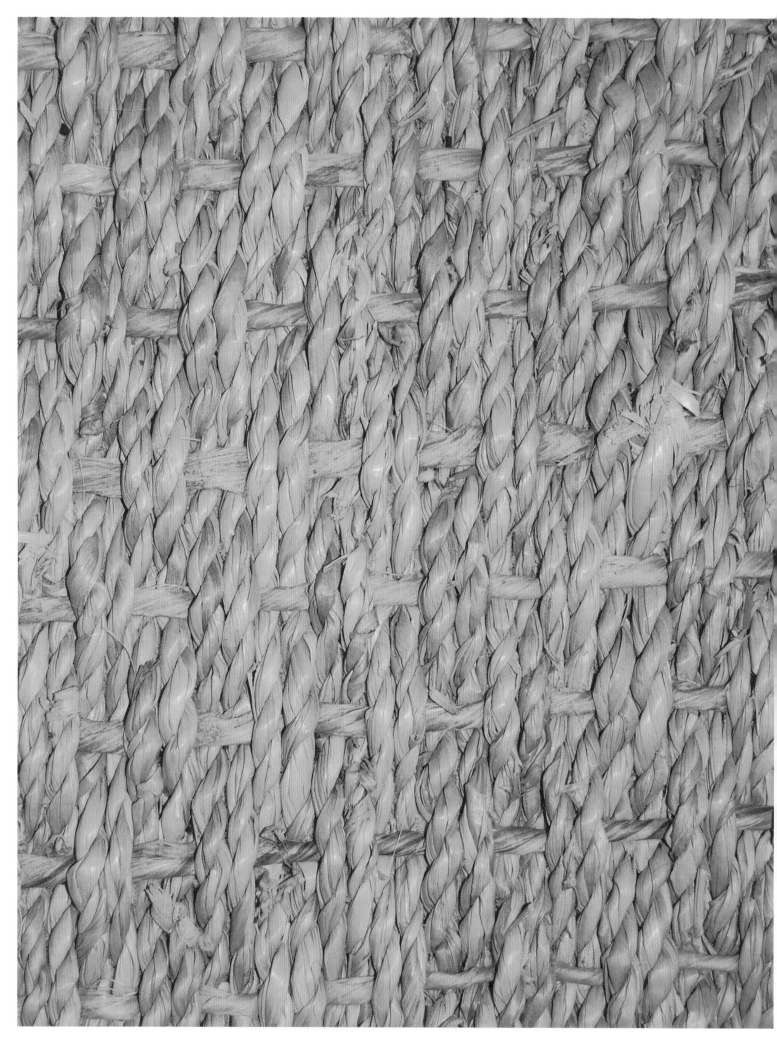

CHAPTER 3 KEY ISSUES TO UNDERSTAND

64 INTRODUCING THE KEY ISSUES

64 ENERGY

78 WATER

84 MATERIALS

107 CONSTRUCTION METHODS

Introducing the key issues

In this chapter, we will set out the effects of building systems, materials, and construction methods on the key environmental issues that we outlined in Chapter 1. We will then explore how to make sustainable design choices about energy and water systems, products, and assemblies for interior projects.

When developing sustainable designs, the main elements to consider are energy and water use, materials, and building techniques. Designers can easily influence these areas through design and specification, and each has a major environmental impact.

Energy, both that used to run a completed interior and that embedded in the products used to make it, has the greatest effect, being the main source of global carbon emissions. Building systems choices primarily affect a project's environmental impact in use, whereas material choices also dictate the environmental impact of delivering a project.

Most energy production results in greenhouse gas emissions, contributing to climate change. Conventional energy consumption also results in resource depletion, as the fossil fuels that the process uses will not be replenished during our lifetimes. It is therefore important to reduce our energy use, through passive design and energy-efficient products, and to choose renewable energy sources.

Water use evidently has a direct influence on water scarcity. Less obviously, the energy associated with processing and transporting clean water means that using water contributes to carbon emissions and, hence, climate change. We can counter this by using water-conserving products, reusing rainwater, and recycling graywater.

Materials have a broader effect on environmental issues, from climate change to resource depletion, biodiversity loss, waste, and health. The energy required through a product's life cycle adds to carbon emissions and climate change, while the impact on other environmental issues varies widely between different materials. In addition, materials affect the functionality of a space, from its durability to its thermal performance, continuing to affect a project's environmental impact once it is in use. Reducing our consumption of materials and reusing or recycling materials are essential to mitigate the damage.

How materials are put together to construct an interior affects their contribution to waste associated with site works, building maintenance, and the eventual demolition of the space. Using prefabricated construction, and assemblies that can easily be dismantled for reuse or recycling, can help.

Energy

As we saw in Chapter 1, energy use in buildings is the main culprit in the construction industry's impact on global carbon emissions. Reducing energy use in their projects is therefore a sensible starting point for the sustainable interior designer. This section will expand on the impacts of energy use and explore how it can be reduced through design. We will discuss passive design, energy-efficient specification, and renewable energy systems, as well as energy-assessment systems.

Impacts of energy use

The environmental effects of energy consumption comprise climate change and resource depletion. The energy we use is usually supplied to our buildings in two forms: electricity and gas.

Since its widespread adoption during the Industrial Revolution in the nineteenth century, most electricity generation has been a dirty process. Today, the majority of power stations continue to burn coal, oil, and natural gas to generate 70% of the world's electricity. This leads to air pollution, in the form of greenhouse gas emissions, which, as well as making the air unpleasant, contribute to climate change. Nuclear power, whereby atomic fission creates electricity, is a cleaner option, and is increasingly replacing fossil fuels as a means to produce energy, especially in the developed world, accounting for 14% of global electricity production.

Yet nuclear generation comes with its own environmental issues: it creates highly dangerous radioactive waste, which must be safely stored for thousands of years; and there is a risk, however slight, of catastrophic environmental disaster, as happened in Chernobyl in 1986, should something go wrong. Of course, oil extraction and transportation also carry the risk of large-scale environmental devastation, exemplified by the infamous marine oil spills off Alaska in 1989 and in the Gulf of Mexico in 2010.

Obtaining coal, oil, natural gas, and uranium to fuel our power stations and satisfy our growing electricity demands leads to resource depletion, as all these resources are finite. Coal, oil, and natural gas are fossil fuels, formed from decaying animal and vegetable matter over millions of years. Reserves are steadily being depleted, so once they are used up we will have no choice but to rely on other methods of energy production. Peak oil and gas are expected to be reached in around 2010 and peak coal at around 2030, after which supplies would decline. Uranium is more abundant, but its availability is by no means infinite. The diminishing availability of fossil fuels is already leading to rising energy prices and fears over energy security. With certain countries having control over the remaining fossil fuel reserves, increasing human conflict over energy supply is almost inevitable.

Wind farms can provide large-scale renewable energy but are not without environmental impacts.

Large-scale renewable energy, such as hydroelectric, wind, and solar power, would solve many of the above problems. Sadly, lack of investment and infrastructure to support renewable energy means it is far from making a significant contribution to meeting our energy needs: hydroelectric supplies 16% of global energy and other renewables a mere 3%. And no electricity production is totally innocuous. For example, wind farms raise concerns about noise, disturbing migrating birds, and spoiling the appearance of the natural landscape.

On top of all this, electricity is an extremely wasteful way of supplying energy. Much energy is lost in converting energy from fuel to electrical energy, transporting electricity from power stations to our buildings, and by inefficient appliances within our buildings. As an extreme example, a conventional domestic incandescent lightbulb converts only 1% of the fossil fuel energy consumed to power it into light.

Gas is a more efficient option than electricity because it is a direct source of energy that does not need to be converted from another form. However, it must still be processed to remove impurities and transported through pipelines. In any case, natural gas is also a finite resource, causing the same concerns as electricity over resource depletion and energy security.

Approaching low-energy design

Clearly, it is imperative that we reduce our energy use and carefully consider its source. This is where designers are well placed to help. Best of all, as all energy use adds to the cost of running a building, few clients are averse to having a low-energy design.

How designers approach low-energy design depends partly on the nature of their role and the project. But there are clear priorities. First, they should seek to reduce energy demand in the building through passive design; next, they should choose energy-efficient products; finally, they should try to ensure that the remaining energy demand comes from a renewable source.

Interior designers working alongside other design consultants may not always be responsible for all these aspects of the design. The building orientation, form, and fabric that dictate passive design might be under an architect's control, while a systems engineer might choose the energy system and appliances used. Regardless of this, the interior designer can make a valuable contribution to the team by suggesting low-energy measures, if equipped with an understanding of the options. The interior designer can further the energy strategies set up by other areas of the design by ensuring that the furniture layout, materials, and equipment complement them. Besides, on small projects where the interior designer is the sole consultant or one of few, these choices could well be within their scope.

The location, type, and duration of the project will also influence what can be done. The building's site and context will dictate what can be achieved through passive design and which energy systems are feasible. For example, a noisy or polluted setting will constrain a passive ventilation strategy reliant on opening windows and open-plan interiors. A heavily shaded site would not suit solar panels and might not require blinds for solar shading. More fundamentally, the local climate will determine whether heating or cooling the interior is the greater priority.

As for project type, a renovation project, especially one in a sensitive historic building, imposes limitations of working within a set structure and energy system. Yet it presents an enormous opportunity to improve the performance of the existing building fabric and systems. The function of the building—including its purpose, hours of use, and number of occupants—will determine how much energy is needed, and when, and which energy system is most suitable. For instance, an office with many staff and computers will have a high cooling demand.

Different considerations will apply to temporary, flexible, and long-term projects. Shorter-term projects should rely as much as possible on passive design, as there will be less time to recoup investment in energy-efficient products or renewable energy. Having said this, temporary projects can be a good means for demonstrating or piloting renewable technologies, for example as part of an exhibition. Flexible projects are designed to accommodate change, either day to day, or to preempt future needs, and are inherently sustainable. This flexibility must be supported by energy choices such as reconfigurable lighting tracks, accessible service routes, and changing light effects. Adaptable projects can also make allowances for renewable technologies, such as solar panels, to be added in future if funding is not available at the outset. In long-term projects, the energy demand in use is critical, as it will define the space's impact for years to come. It is easier to justify using on-site renewable energy and the most energy-efficient products, as running efficiencies will ultimately pay off the investment. An added challenge is to design the space to cope with the effects of climate change that are anticipated within its lifetime. This could include a greater need for cooling and flood defences in the northern hemisphere, and greater precautions against drought in the southern hemisphere.

TIP ENERGY-SAVING INFORMATION

Consult websites such as that of the Energy Saving Trust for details of energy-saving measures and renewable energy systems:

www.energysavingtrust.org.uk

STEP BY STEP LOW-ENERGY DESIGN

When designing a low-energy interior it is sensible to follow the priorities of passive design, then energy efficiency, then renewable energy. Here we see how the principle can be applied to lighting design:

1 Passive design is the first measure to consider. Making the most of daylight to reduce the need for electric lighting is one example.

2 Energy efficiency is the next priority and might involve installing low-energy lightbulbs to ensure that electricity is used efficiently.

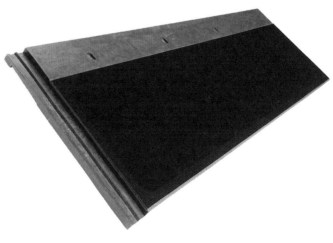

3 Renewable energy can be considered next, perhaps by incorporating photovoltaic panels to meet electricity needs.

Passive design

Employing passive design strategies is the simplest and most effective way in which a designer can minimize the energy required by their project. As we saw in Chapter 1, passive design means manipulating the building's orientation, shape, layout, and envelope to take advantage of natural energy from the sun, wind, outside temperature, and building occupants. It requires no technology and is therefore free energy. Of course, some passive design measures will not be possible on certain sites and in existing buildings where previous designers have already made the key decisions about the building.

As passive design is simple and effective, it should be prioritized over active technologies, such as renewable energy systems. It makes sense to get the most from passive design before seeking extra benefits from technology. The principles of passive design are readily understood, allowing designers to easily incorporate it in their projects.

The principal passive design measures are solar gain, solar shading, thermal mass, thermal insulation, natural ventilation, air-tightness, and natural daylighting. Living walls can also contribute to a passive design strategy.

Solar gain This means using the sun's heat to warm interior spaces, reducing or eliminating the need for mechanical heating in cooler climates. The effect is achieved by using the amount and orientation of glazing to allow in heat from the sun during the day. In the northern hemisphere, large panes of south-facing glazing will let in most sun; in the southern hemisphere, the opposite applies. For best results, this should be combined with high thermal mass and smaller openings on the other walls to store the heat. Interior designers should ensure that the internal layout places appropriate activities in the sunny spaces and does not block the sun unnecessarily.

Solar shading To control solar gain, avoiding summer overheating and glare, solar shading should be provided in the form of external louvers, deep overhangs, solar-control glazing, or interstitial blinds. Indeed, solar shading is a useful passive strategy in itself to prevent solar gain in warmer climates. To get the most from solar gain, designers should consider the heating need, the availability of sunshine on the site, the sun's path around the site, and the angle of the sun throughout the year. The sun moves from the east across the meridian to the west during the day, and is much higher in the sky in summer than in winter. As well as reducing energy use, controlled sunshine can have a positive effect on our mood.

Right
Plan showing passive solar strategy for Jestico + Whiles's House for the Future in Cardiff (UK). The house's south-facing glazing admits the sun's heat as it passes from east to west in the northern hemisphere. The north of the house incorporates solid earth walls, providing thermal mass, to capture the heat.

Bottom right
This section shows how the House for the Future captures the sun's energy. Glass allows the low winter sun in to warm the interior; the sloped roof shields the living spaces from the high summer sun and has solar panels.

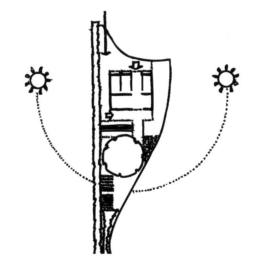

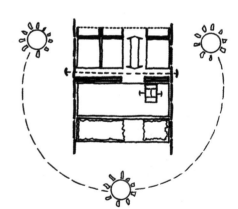

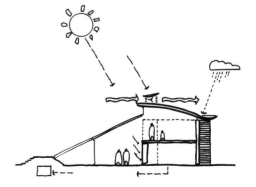

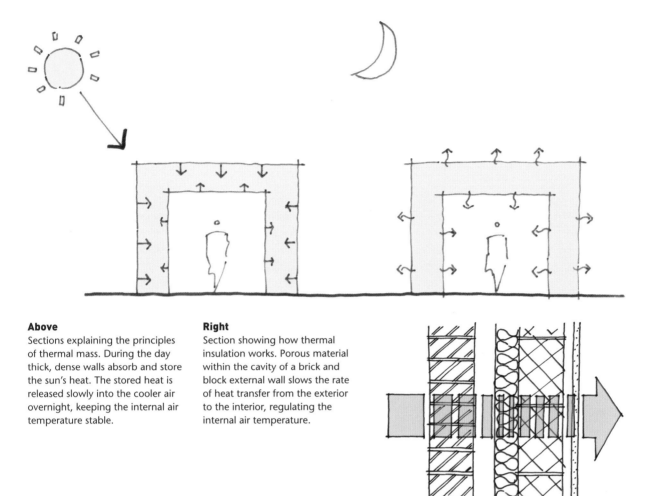

Above
Sections explaining the principles of thermal mass. During the day thick, dense walls absorb and store the sun's heat. The stored heat is released slowly into the cooler air overnight, keeping the internal air temperature stable.

Right
Section showing how thermal insulation works. Porous material within the cavity of a brick and block external wall slows the rate of heat transfer from the exterior to the interior, regulating the internal air temperature.

Thermal mass Designers can use dense materials with high heat capacity to provide thermal mass. Thermal mass stores heat or coolness and transfers it slowly into the space to keep the internal temperature reasonably constant, reducing the need for artificial heating or cooling. Suitable materials include thick masonry, concrete, rammed earth, or brickwork, and should be exposed to the interior or finished with conductive materials such as ceramic tiles. The use of thermal mass needs to vary to suit the climate. In hot, dry climates, it is best used for the external walls, roof, and floor to help keep the space cooler than the outside air. In cooler climates, it is best used on internal surfaces exposed to solar gain, as explained above, to capture heat from the sun. The benefits of thermal mass must be balanced against the potentially higher embodied energy of the construction required, partly attributed to transporting the heavy materials, making this strategy best suited to longer-term projects.

Thermal insulation This is distinct from thermal mass but can also reduce the need for mechanical heating and cooling. It involves using materials that reduce the rate of heat transfer on the external envelope to ensure that the internal air temperature responds slowly to changes in external temperature. This works in both hot and cold climates, keeping the space warmer or cooler than the outside air. Insulating pipework and storage tanks for hot water within the building is also important to avoid heat losses. Highly insulating materials tend to be porous, trapping air, which is a poor heat conductor. Typical examples are sheep's wool, mineral wool, and cellulose fibers, while high-performance glazing can mitigate heat losses or gains through openings. Even in renovation projects, the interior designer can use insulating materials to line the inner faces of the external envelope and upgrade glazing to ameliorate thermal performance. Insulation must be balanced with ventilation to control humidity. The interior designer should weigh up the performance of an insulation product against other environmental considerations, which we will cover in the section on materials.

Natural ventilation This involves using the position of openings—be they windows, roof lights, air vents, or chimneys—to encourage air flow through a space. This replenishes fresh air and prevents overheating, reducing or avoiding the need for mechanical ventilation. There are two main forms: cross-ventilation and stack ventilation. Cross-ventilation uses openings on opposite sides of a room to let natural breezes in and out. The convection effect of hot air rising is exploited in stack ventilation, using openings at low level to admit cooler air and at high level to extract warmer air. External noise, pollution, and wind patterns will govern whether natural ventilation will be effective. Occupants often feel better in naturally ventilated spaces, especially if they have control over their environment by opening and closing windows.

Air-tightness Natural ventilation needs to be reconciled with air-tightness, which is needed to avoid unwanted heat loss and drafts. All gaps in construction, particularly in the external fabric, should be tightly sealed with close-fitting joints and sealant to maintain the integrity of the envelope. This need not preclude natural ventilation, providing it is controlled through closable openings and combined with breathable construction that allows air to pass through. In some cases, low-energy mechanical ventilation may be a better solution to allow maximum air-tightness and control humidity.

Section showing cross-ventilation. Windows on either side of a shallow, open-plan interior allow breezes to travel through the space, providing natural cooling and ventilation.

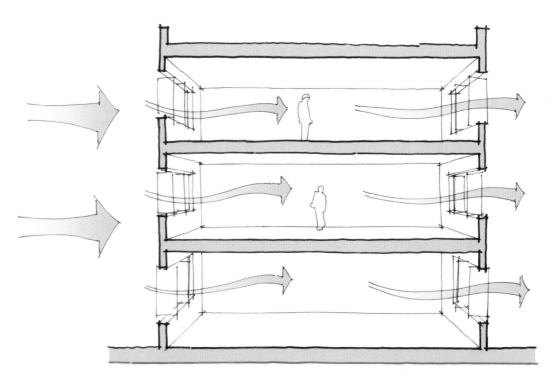

Natural daylighting The depth of rooms and amount of glazing, or other transparent materials, can be modified to optimize natural daylighting, reducing the need for electric lighting. Shallow rooms with plenty of windows will let in most daylight. Similarly, using transparent, translucent, or reflective materials indoors increases penetration of daylight within the interior. Further, an interior can be planned so that desks and other areas needing most light are located near windows or roof lights. As indicated above, the effects of large amounts of external glazing on heat loss and solar gain should be considered when developing the daylighting strategy. Daylight and associated views promote the health and well-being of the building's occupants.

Living walls Lastly, living walls are a useful passive measure and can be used indoors. Those including soil provide thermal mass, while the plants also absorb air pollution and dust. Having plants in the built environment also creates a symbolic link to nature, reminding us of our connection with and enjoyment of the natural world.

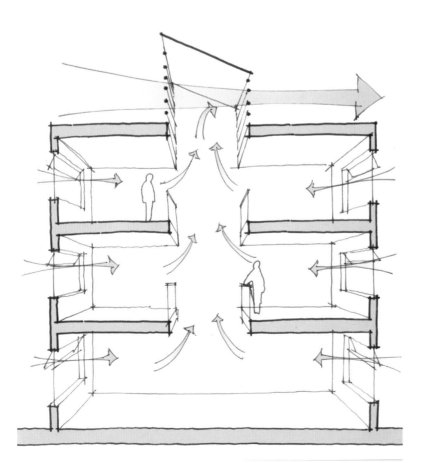

Above
This indoor living wall, created by Patrick Blanc for the Natural History Museum in Toulouse (France), contributes to good air quality and acts as a reminder of the natural world.

Left
Section showing stack ventilation. A tall atrium, open at the top and to each floor, allows warm, stale air to rise out of the building. Replacement fresh air is admitted through opening windows on each floor level, naturally cooling and ventilating the interior.

Energy efficiency

Once all possible passive design measures have been exhausted, the interior designer's attention can turn to energy efficiency. This can range from choosing energy-efficient lighting, appliances, and building systems to influencing occupant behavior by including metering and convenient switches.

Lighting Compact fluorescent lightbulbs and light-emitting diodes (LEDs) are good examples of energy-efficient lighting, which use less energy than standard lightbulbs to produce the same amount of light. The selection of low-energy light fixtures is rapidly increasing; they give impressive results and typically last much longer than their energy-guzzling counterparts. Efficient lighting can be linked to movement sensors, daylight sensors, or timers to ensure that the lights come on only when needed. Interior designers should plan lighting zones and locate switches to make it easy for the building's users to turn lights off in each part of the space.

Low-energy lighting comes in many forms, including these Sparks LED light fixtures designed by Daniel Becker Design Studio.

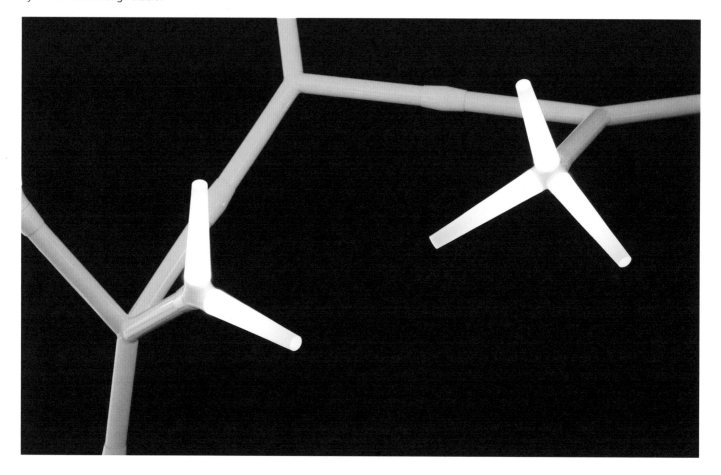

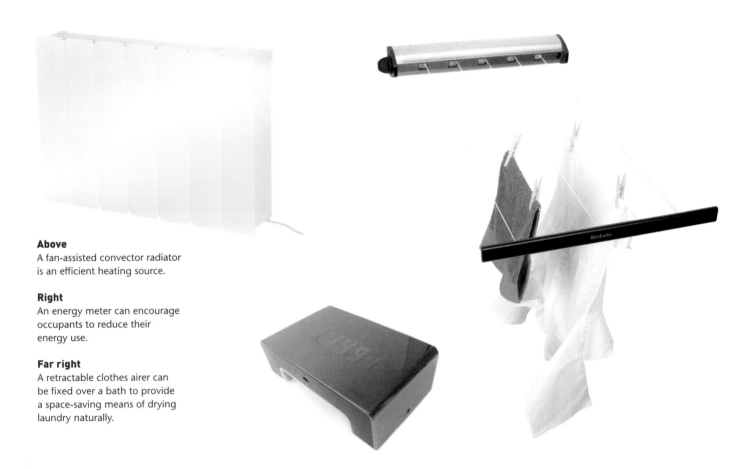

Above
A fan-assisted convector radiator
is an efficient heating source.

Right
An energy meter can encourage
occupants to reduce their
energy use.

Far right
A retractable clothes airer can
be fixed over a bath to provide
a space-saving means of drying
laundry naturally.

Appliances As with lighting, energy-efficient appliances use less energy to achieve the same performance as other models. The main appliances a designer might select include refrigerators, freezers, washing machines, dryers, and dishwashers. Again, energy-efficient appliances are widely available.

Building systems Energy-efficient building systems are readily available to provide heating, ventilation, and cooling. Efficient heating options include condensing or combination boilers, underfloor or in-slab pipework, and fan-assisted convector radiators. Condensing and combination boilers capture the heat that is normally lost as waste gases. Underfloor and pipe-in-slab heating systems work at low temperatures as they distribute heat evenly throughout a space. Underfloor heating has the added advantage of delivering the heat at low level, close to the building's occupants. Fan-assisted convector radiators use a fan to improve heat delivery and distribution compared with conventional radiators. Thermostats and timers should be used with the heating system to ensure that heat output does not exceed demand. Occupants can be encouraged to turn off heating when not needed through logical planning of heating zones and controls.

Ventilation systems can include heat recovery, efficient fan motors, and automatic controls to optimize their efficiency. Heat-recovery ventilation reuses the waste heat it extracts from the space to warm incoming air. Efficient fan motors simply minimize the energy needed to power the system. Automatic controls detect air pollution, humidity, and occupancy levels and adjust the ventilation rates accordingly.

If cooling is essential, it is important to choose an energy-efficient air-conditioning system. However, it is worth noting that air-conditioning systems contain chemical refrigerants. These substances contribute to global warming and the depletion of the Earth's protective ozone layer, increasing our exposure to harmful ultraviolet radiation. The more damaging chlorofluorocarbon (CFC) and hydrochlorofluorocarbon (HCFC) refrigerants are banned or being phased out in many countries, including those in the European Union; the alternatives, hydrofluorocarbons (HFCs) or hydrocarbons (HCs), have no ozone depletion potential (ODP) and comparatively modest global warming potential (GWP).

Influencing behavior Finally, other simple measures can encourage the building's users to use energy efficiently. Introducing energy meters and prominent energy displays helps occupants see how much energy they are using and take the initiative to reduce it. Similarly, providing the space and equipment to dry clothes naturally gives people a convenient alternative to inefficient dryers.

Renewable energy systems

Renewable energy systems are the next thing to consider, after passive design and energy efficiency have been incorporated. They produce energy from renewable sources, rather than finite sources like fossil fuels. Small-scale renewable energy can be generated on site, eliminating the inefficiencies of transporting electricity, and can provide heating or power. Some systems have a high capital cost, although grants are often available. Besides, once the technology is in place to generate it, the energy is free and will make up for the capital cost over time—in fact, any excess energy can usually be sold to the national grid.

The most common small-scale renewable energy technologies are biomass, wind power, solar thermal heating, photovoltaic cells (PVs), and heat pumps. All of these come with particular design requirements and considerations, which are described below.

Biomass This involves burning natural fuel, such as wood pellets, to provide heating. Biomass can consist of a room stove for local heating or a boiler feeding a central heating system. Designers must include an exhaust flue, adequate space for fuel storage, and access for fuel deliveries. It is essential to consider where the fuel comes from, choosing a supplier that guarantees the wood pellets derive from sustainable sources or industrial waste. After all, growing biofuel could potentially divert land from food crops or contribute to deforestation.

Wind power A wind turbine can be used to convert wind energy into electricity. Clearly, wind conditions on site will govern whether wind power is viable, and on any site wind will be a variable, unreliable presence. For these reasons, wind power is most successful in rural settings with domestic-scale energy demands. Turbines need to be reasonably large and high up to work efficiently, so they have a definite visual impact, and they can be noisy.

Solar thermal heating Solar thermal collectors harness heat from the sun for water heating by warming roof-mounted panels containing tubes or flat plates and storing the hot water in a hot-water cylinder. They work best at the orientation and angle that will receive most sunshine (due south in the northern hemisphere; due north in the southern hemisphere); the angle depends on the site's latitude. The panels should be sited to avoid overshadowing by buildings or trees. As solar panels are relatively easy to retrofit, they are a valid option for renovation projects.

Photovoltaic cells The sun's heat can also be converted into electricity, using PVs. These are panels containing semiconducting material that triggers an electrical field when sunlight shines through it. These are generally roof-mounted, although wall panels exist. The optimum angle and orientation, and the need to avoid overshadowing, are the same as for solar thermal panels; retrofitting is equally viable for PVs.

Heat pumps These are classified as renewable energy, although they do require some external power to operate the pump. To be truly renewable, PVs or a green energy supplier can provide this additional power. Heat pumps can be ground-, water-, or air-based and provide space heating and cooling. The first two types exploit the fairly constant temperature of the subsoil or deep water, such as an aquifer, which varies little throughout the day and year. Water mixed with antifreeze is piped underground to be warmed or cooled by the earth or water, then piped back to feed a central heating and cooling system. Air-source heat pumps extract heat from the outside air, through heat exchange, to warm water or air for space heating. Heat pumps are best combined with underfloor heating or fan-assisted convector radiators, since both operate at low temperatures. The site must have suitable ground conditions or a water body to support a ground- or water-source heat pump, but, as the pipes can run horizontally or vertically, even under the building, lack of space need not be a constraint.

An alternative way of supporting renewable energy is to use a commercial renewable energy supplier. However, it is important to note that tenants in sublet buildings tend to have the right to change their energy supplier. Note that it is better to choose a supplier that invests only in renewable energy than one that simply offers a green tariff to meet its legal obligations.

Energy assessment

Being able to assess energy performance can be a valuable tool for an interior designer, helping them check their assumptions, decide between products, and convince clients of the merit of low-energy design. Chapter 2 showed that energy is routinely considered as part of any whole-design assessment process, but it is also possible to evaluate energy use in isolation. This can be particularly useful for verifying the effectiveness of passive design measures and energy efficiency.

Passive design can be checked by calculation during the design stage and post-completion testing. At the design stage, tools such as daylight and u-value calculators allow designers to input basic data to estimate whether their projects will provide enough daylight and insulation, respectively. More sophisticated computer modeling software can be used to establish how much sunlight and ventilation will reach the interior and how much carbon the design will account for.

After completion, possible tests to check that the actual performance meets the design intent include air-pressure tests for air-tightness and smoke tests for natural ventilation. Energy performance certificates, which are compulsory for housing sales and public buildings in countries like the UK, rate the building's energy performance against a standard benchmark. In addition, initiatives such as the UK's Carbon Buzz, run by BRE and the Royal Institute of British Architects (RIBA), allow designers to compare their projects' designed and actual energy use.

LINK www.carbonbuzz.org

Many certification systems are in place to rate the energy efficiency of products, making it easy for designers to choose the best performing models. In Europe, the EU Energy Label Scheme is compulsory for lighting and appliances, which are rated from A++, A+, or A to G. Other marks of energy-efficient products include Cleaner and Greener, and Green-e, which apply worldwide; Energy Saving Recommended, One Planet Products, Group for Efficient Appliances Label, and The Environment Tree in Europe; Energy Star and Eco Options in North America; Energy Star in New Zealand; Energy Rating Program in Australia; and Energy Saving Labelling Program in Asia. Renewable energy products are also covered by various certification systems, such as TUV Mark, Eugene Green Energy Standard, GreenPower, and 100% Green Electricity.

Biomass stoves can provide a renewable source of energy and an elegant focal point in a room. The stoves burn natural fuel, such as wood pellets, to provide a local heat source.

TIP ENERGY LABELS

Check the energy label on lighting and appliances to choose an efficient model. Seek products with an A, A+, or A++ rating. The Global Ecolabelling Network's website has details of energy labels used worldwide:

www.ecolabelling.org

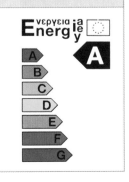

Case study Low-energy design

Courtyard House, Los Angeles (US) by Ripple Design

Above
With the doors closed, the interior is sealed from the courtyard for warmth. Deep roof overhangs and low-emissivity glazing control solar gain.

Above right
With the doors fully open to the courtyard, the interior is cooled by breezes.

Below
The orientation and steeply sloping ceilings capture breezes to aid ventilation. Thick exposed concrete, stucco, and masonry walls and ceilings provide thermal mass.

Ripple Design's Courtyard House in Los Angeles combines passive design, energy efficiency, and renewable energy systems to create a low-energy design. The fact that the project is new-build, and combines architecture and interior design, enabled the energy strategy to be comprehensive.

The passive strategies center on the courtyard typology, a traditional solution for dry, coastal areas. The main living areas can be fully opened to an internal courtyard, thanks to their retractable doors and sliding windows, giving the inhabitants a sense of living outdoors. The occupants thus control how open the interior is to the courtyard to regulate the internal temperature and ventilation. The form and orientation of the house accentuate the effect, acting as a scoop to collect cool westerly sea breezes and draw them through a chimney with openable roof lights, providing passive stack ventilation. The orientation, sloping roofs, and deep roof overhangs also control solar gains in the interior.

Inside, thick walls and ceilings made of dense materials, such as exposed concrete, stucco, and masonry, provide thermal mass in locations where they will absorb the sun's heat and release it gradually. In combination with rooms that are embedded into the sloping site, high-performance insulation and low-emissivity glazing, this stabilizes internal temperatures and avoids the need for air conditioning. Reflective internal surfaces distribute daylight from the courtyard around the interior, minimizing the need for artificial light.

Energy-saving products include a highly efficient boiler and underfloor heating.

On-site renewable systems, in the form of photovoltaic and solar-thermal roof panels, supply all the home's energy needs, with any surplus being fed back into the grid.

Reflective surfaces, such as light-colored wood, maximize natural daylight.

Water

Chapter 1 illustrated the adverse effects of water use in buildings on core environmental issues. In this section we will elaborate on these effects and discuss how the interior designer can mitigate them. We will cover passive design, water-saving products, water reuse and recycling, and assessment of water efficiency.

Impacts of water use

As well as directly compounding water scarcity, our use of clean water has an indirect effect on climate change and fuel depletion.

Water use obviously heightens problems of water scarcity, especially in dry countries or during periods of drought. It is already a challenge to source sufficient clean water in some countries, such as southern Australia. Climate change, which is likely to increase the frequency of drought in many parts of the world, and population growth, will only exacerbate this.

Lack of available water results in rationing how much people can use or dictating what they can use it for. This causes inconvenience or even suffering, diverts water from agriculture, and potentially triggers conflict between people.

Despite this, in the developed world we are each using more and more water for drinking and for daily activities such as cooking, personal washing, clothes washing, cleaning, and growing plants. Global water demand has increased by twice the rate of population growth over the past century. Desalination—treating sea water to increase the supply of drinking water—offers a possible solution. However, the process is expensive, energy-intensive, and potentially damaging to marine habitats.

Processing fresh water to make it potable requires energy; therefore our clean water has embodied carbon, and so contributes to climate change and fossil-fuel depletion. In addition, water treatment uses potent chemicals, such as chlorine, which must be carefully disposed of to avoid pollution of surrounding ecosystems.

Modern buildings use the potable water supply, rather than a separate tank, for both drinking water and plumbing fixtures. Yet it is arguably extravagant to use drinking-quality water for washing clothes, flushing toilets, and watering plants.

As we cover the ground with more and more hard surfaces, rainwater runs directly into our sewerage system, rather than soaking into the ground to complete the natural water cycle. This can overload the drainage system, causing flooding and pollution, and requiring unnecessary water treatment.

Paradoxically, water abundance is also a growing problem, with global warming expected to increase the likelihood of flooding in many areas, affecting developments near flood plains and the coast.

Approaching water-conserving design

To solve these problems, it is vital to reduce our water consumption and consider flood risk. Interior designers can encourage water conservation and, where water is metered, offer consequent savings in running costs to clients or their tenants.

For water conservation, the priorities are comparable to those for low-energy design. Passive design should be considered first, followed by water efficiency, then water reuse or recycling. To deal with flooding, designers should favor flood prevention over flood protection measures.

The interior designer's role on the project will have a bearing on what they can do. However, they can always make suggestions to the architect, landscape architect, or systems engineer when working within a team, and must ensure that their input enhances any sustainable measures proposed by these consultants. While passive design measures involve manipulating the landscaping and roof, which is seldom within an interior designer's remit, the interior designer will often choose plumbing fixtures, appliances, and faucets, which determine water efficiency.

The location, type, and duration of the project must also be taken into account. The amount of rainfall the site receives will govern whether rainwater collection is worthwhile. Water conservation is important on all projects and is simple to incorporate. But the longer the project is expected to last, the more critical water saving becomes, as the building will continue to affect water use for years to come. Equally, longer-term projects need especially to heed the effects of climate change, and consider drought and flood protection in high-risk areas. Long-term designs can allow for technologies like rainwater reuse to be retrofitted in future if funds are not available at the outset.

Although a renovation or fit-out project places constraints on the designer through its fixed structure and systems, there may be huge scope to improve water efficiency in the existing building. A building's use is also important in assessing water demand and whether water reuse or recycling are suitable. For example, a hotel where bathrooms are stacked above each other is ideal for gravity-based graywater recycling.

STEP BY STEP WATER-CONSERVING DESIGN

Designers should apply the priorities of passive design, then water efficiency, then water reuse or recycling when aiming for a water-conserving design:

1 Passive design should be the first priority. Installing a rainwater butt for watering plants, thereby reducing the demand for clean water, is a simple solution.

2 Water efficiency should be tackled next, for example, by specifying water-efficient faucets that ensure water is used economically.

3 Lastly, water reuse or recycling can be incorporated in the interior, reducing the need for clean water. One option is a combined WC and washbasin that recycles graywater from the basin to flush the toilet.

Passive design

Passive design addresses water issues by tuning the form and materials of the building and its site to take advantage of rainfall and control rainwater runoff. Useful passive design strategies include rainwater collection, sustainable drainage, and planting.

Rainwater can be captured by designing the roofs and rainwater drainage to discharge into water stores. These stores range from domestic water butts at the end of a rainwater pipe to large underground tanks. The stored water can be used directly to water plants, including indoor plants, if the store has a faucet, reducing demand for potable water. Alternatively, it might form part of a more active rainwater reuse system, as described below.

Sustainable drainage systems are especially relevant to built-up areas with mainly hard surfaces, where rainwater runoff can trigger flooding and spread pollutants. Hence, they are often termed Sustainable Urban Drainage Systems (SUDS). At their simplest, SUDS constitute substituting porous materials, such as gravel, permeable paving, and areas of planting for typical hard surfacing outside the building, to allow rainwater to trickle through to the soil below. This reduces runoff and avoids the spread of pollutants from hard surfaces. More complex SUDS convey rainwater to a pond or an underground store. In either form, SUDS will avoid flooding in the landscape and reduce the risk of floodwater reaching the interior.

As well as helping with SUDS at ground level, planting can help when used in green roofs and living walls. The plants and soil absorb rainwater, slowing runoff. Locating planting where it receives rainfall and choosing native plants, which are suited to the local climate, will reduce the demand on water for irrigation. Moreover, the native species provide a particularly valuable habitat for wildlife, encouraging biodiversity.

Water efficiency

Water efficiency is the next priority after passive design and is typically where the interior designer can contribute most to a water-conserving design. To this end, they can choose water-saving plumbing fixtures and appliances, and suggest water meters to encourage responsible use of water by the building's occupants.

Water-saving plumbing fixtures These fixtures use less water than standard products without compromising performance. Water-efficient alternatives are widely available for faucets, showers, baths, toilets, and urinals.

Automatic faucets, which use infrared sensors to release water only when someone places their hands below them, are commonly used to prevent water being wasted by a running faucet. Spray faucets have small perforations, instead of a single opening, to release a fine mist of water and give good coverage while limiting the flow of water; aerated faucets boost the power of the water by combining it with air.

For a similar effect, water-conserving showers limit and aerate water flow through the shower head, which reduces water use by as much as 75% compared with an ordinary shower. Other water-saving showers spray jets of water together to enhance coverage.

Dual-flush toilets have two flush settings, giving the building occupants control over how much water they need. Composting toilets are a more radical option, using little or no water. They typically decompose and dehydrate human waste in a sealed container to produce compost that can be used on the garden.

Waterless urinals rely on a urine-repellent coating, an efficient shape for drainage, and a disposable trap seal to remove urine and its odor without the need for water. A waterless urinal saves on average 40,000 gallons (150,000 liters) of water per year.

Low-volume baths are molded on the inside to allow a deep bath that saves around 24 gallons (90 liters) of water compared with a standard bath.

Water-saving appliances Appliances can also be chosen for their water efficiency. When specifying washing machines and dishwashers, interior designers can select models that use less water than typical models. The best-performing washing machines use under 1 gallon of water per pound (7.5 liters per kilogram), while the worst use up to 5 gallons (20 liters); efficient dishwashers use less than ¼ gallon (1 liter) of water per place setting, while inefficient ones can exceed ¾ gallon (3 liters).

Water meters Lastly, installing a water meter in the interior or specific zones of the interior allows the occupants to see how much water they are using, encouraging them to use it sparingly. Shower meters and timers can be installed locally to show people how much water they are using and alert them when they reach a recommended limit.

Left
Water-conserving showers restrict water use without inhibiting performance.

Below left
A dual-flush toilet has two flush settings that release different amounts of water.

Right
Urinals that avoid the use of water altogether are available. They are shaped to optimize drainage and coated to repel urine, eliminating the need to flush with water.

Below
Low-volume baths are molded to fit the human body and thus use minimal water for a deep bath.

Left
A shower meter can encourage people to use less water when showering.

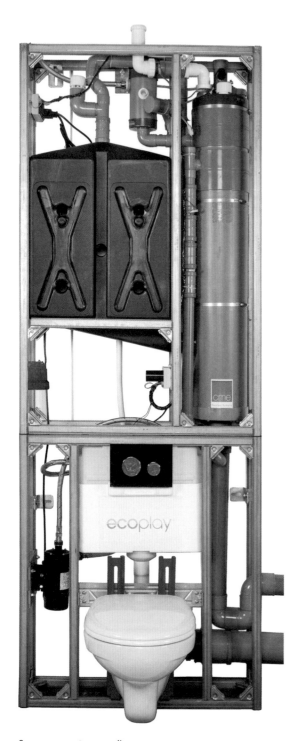

Some graywater recycling systems rely on gravity, avoiding the energy use associated with a pump. This compact system, which is concealed behind the toilet pan, contains a cleaning tank that collects waste water from a bathroom on the floor above. A storage tank below retains the cleaned water, while a control unit monitors water quality and use, automatically draining excess water before it becomes stale.

Water reuse and recycling

Water reuse and recycling can be used to support passive design, as indicated above, or as an additional measure. It involves collecting rainwater from outside or waste water from within the building to use for another purpose on the site. This reduces the demand for potable water from the mains supply.

Water reuse and recycling falls into three categories: rainwater reuse, graywater recycling, and blackwater recycling. They should be considered in that order, which reflects their ease of implementation.

Rainwater reuse Rainwater can be collected by the passive methods outlined above and used to flush toilets, feed washing machines, or water plants. These systems can supply as much as half of a typical household's water needs. Rainwater is beneficial to plants as, unlike drinking water, it contains the nutrients they need and is at external air temperature. Watering cans can be filled directly from a faucet in a rainwater butt, or a rainwater storage tank can be connected to an irrigation system. For flushing toilets and supplying washing machines, the rainwater is filtered and piped into the cistern or appliance. Depending on where the rainwater is stored, a pump may be required to direct it to its point of use, so the energy implications of this should be taken into account.

Graywater recycling This means collecting and reusing waste water from showers, baths, washbasins, and washing machines, and can reduce water use by as much as 30%. Once filtered and treated, this can be used to flush toilets or water nonedible plants. Again, a pump may be needed to transport the water from store to point of use, using energy. However, smart systems exploit gravity to use graywater collected on an upper floor to flush toilets on the floor below.

Blackwater recycling Recycling blackwater is far more drastic and will be desirable only for specific projects— perhaps in remote rural areas where a sewerage system is unavailable—due to the associated cost, maintenance, and odor. It concerns filtering and treating waste water from toilets, dishwashers, and refuse chutes, through a system of tanks or reed beds. The treated water is reused in an underground irrigation system, which waters and fertilizes nonedible plants from below. The reed bed system also provides a habitat for wildlife.

Flood protection

On long-term projects situated in areas prone to flooding, the interior designer would be wise to incorporate flood-protection measures to minimize damage to the interior in the event of a flood. These comprise raised entrance thresholds, water-resistant flooring and baseboards, and plinths for electrical appliances. It is worth noting that many of these features can also be retrofitted if flood risk increases over time.

Water assessment

Assessing water use can help the interior designer understand the impact of their choices and convince the client of potential water savings. Water consumption can be assessed on its own or, as detailed in Chapter 2, as part of a whole-design assessment.

To check the contribution of passive design, calculations can establish how much rain can be collected from a given area of roof, or how much can be diverted from runoff by SUDS (see page 80).

Water efficiency can be checked with reference to the manufacturer's published data or, more conveniently, by choosing products that have been labeled as water-saving by certification bodies such as Waterwise, Water Efficient Product Labelling Scheme, One Planet Products, and The Environment Tree in Europe; WaterSense in North America; Water Efficiency Labelling Stamp (WELS) in Australia; and China Water Conservation Certification in Asia.

Sophisticated rainwater-recycling systems use a large storage tank, either underground or within the building, which can supply irrigation pipes, toilets, or washing machines.

TIP WATER-SAVING INFORMATION

Consult websites such as Waterwise for details of water-saving measures and certified water-saving products: www.waterwise.org.uk

The Global Ecolabelling Network's website provides information on water-saving labels worldwide: www.ecolabelling.org

Materials

Construction materials have wide-ranging and complex effects on the environment, and are clearly the area in which interior designers can have most influence on sustainable design. In this section, we will investigate why specifying sustainable materials is important and how interior designers should approach the process. We will discuss how to minimize the environmental impact of materials and how to assess their merits, taking into account their whole life cycle. Finally, we will discuss how to choose sustainable materials for different purposes and highlight useful databases for sourcing low-impact products.

Impacts of materials

The materials we choose to build with can aggravate resource depletion, climate change, water scarcity, biodiversity loss, waste, and even our health, as well as causing pollution during production.

The most straightforward effect of using materials is resource depletion. Many natural materials are finite or regenerate very slowly. We have seen in the energy section that fossil fuels are finite; it follows that virgin materials derived from fossil fuels, namely plastics, will ultimately run out. Metals are also finite, with global reserves of lead, zinc, and copper projected to run out within the next half-century if present mining rates continue. Stone is formed in the natural geological cycle over thousands and millions of years, and we are quarrying stone at a rate much faster than it will be replaced. Although stone remains abundant, supplies from particular quarries will gradually dwindle—

and leave the landscape scarred. In the UK, for example, availability of virgin slate is already fairly low.

Although a renewable material, wood is replenished slowly, as trees take many years to grow to maturity. This is particularly true of tropical hardwoods. Some 10% of the world's tree species are endangered, and mahogany, sapele, and some species of walnut are classed as vulnerable. Unless forests are managed to ensure that new growth balances felling and only abundant, faster-growing species are cut down, our trees will eventually disappear. On top of depleting our source of wooden products and fuel, deforestation leads to loss of habitat for wildlife, including endangered species, such as orang-utans in Borneo and tigers in Sumatra. Further, removing trees causes topsoil erosion once the soil becomes exposed to wind and rain, harming marine ecosystems and making the soil unproductive. The depletion of our forests also diminishes their capacity to absorb carbon dioxide from the atmosphere, aggravating climate change.

Using materials has an indirect impact on climate change, thanks to the energy used during their life cycle. This is called embodied energy and describes the energy necessary to obtain, process, manufacture, transport, install, maintain, demolish, and dispose of a material. For instance, a stone component must be blasted from a quarry, driven to a factory, cut and honed into panels, driven to the building site, and fixed into position, just to realize one aspect of the project. Once the project is in use, the panel will need to be periodically cleaned, repaired,

Quarrying stone involves the excavation of large areas of unspoiled land, scarring the surrounding landscape. Stone is a finite resource, so supplies from some quarries are running low.

or replaced. And when it is no longer needed, the panel must be dismantled and transported for reuse, recycling, or disposal in landfill. Fuel is essential at every stage of this long process and, consequently, the stone panel contributes to carbon emissions and climate change. In the main, natural materials need less intensive processing and therefore have lower embodied energy than man-made alternatives. For example, vinyl (or PVC) has higher embodied energy than linoleum. However, importing natural materials significantly increases their embodied energy.

Materials have embodied water in the same way as they have embodied energy, as water is used at most stages of a material's life cycle. Thus, using materials contributes to water scarcity. Again, how much water is needed to produce a material depends greatly on the material in question; natural materials, which require less processing, are likely to need less. One exception is cotton, as its production accounts for nearly 3% of global water use. Cotton is often grown for export in countries where access to clean water is already problematic. Water is needed first to irrigate the cotton plants, and then to process the cotton crop into finished fabric by bleaching, dyeing, printing, and finishing. In addition, the fertilizers, pesticides, and chemicals used during production pollute watercourses.

Materials used by the construction industry have a major impact on waste. As we saw in Chapter 1, waste puts pressure on land use and triggers pollution, including emissions of greenhouse gases that cause climate change. Construction waste is caused by demolition of existing buildings and spaces, over-ordering of new materials for building sites, inefficient manufacturing processes, and failure to design to standard modules. For instance, a perfectly serviceable interior might be overhauled and replaced with new materials to fit the latest trend, without a thought for reusing the existing materials. Ceramic tiles might be ordered in excess to suit standard batch sizes, benefit from bulk discounts or avoid the risk of running out if there is a long lead time from ordering to delivery.

Lastly, the materials that interior designers choose can affect our own health and well-being. Off-gassing from VOCs contained in many finishes, adhesives, and furnishings causes internal air pollution. Along with dust and mold, which certain materials and conditions aggravate, air pollution is linked to Sick Building Syndrome and asthma. The Aerias Air Quality Sciences Center's website is a useful resource on indoor air quality.

LINK www.aerias.org

Although cotton fields look idyllic and natural, conventional cotton production is responsible for pollution and intensive water use.

STEP BY STEP CERAMIC TILE LIFE CYCLE

All materials have environmental impacts at every stage of their life cycle: when obtained, processed, manufactured, transported, installed, maintained, and demolished. Ceramic tile manufacturer Royal Mosa has gained Cradle to Cradle certification for its glossy and unglazed tiles by addressing the whole life cycle of its products, as described below. The company is accredited to the ISO 14001 environmental management system.

1 Obtain: The tiles contain between 10 and 40% recycled content, along with natural raw materials from local quarries; 80% of its raw materials are sourced within 250 miles (400km) of the factory.

2 Process: The company has significantly reduced dust emissions during production.

3 Manufacture: Renewable hydroelectric energy powers the factories, contributing to a 17% reduction in carbon emissions. All tile waste and most waste water within the factories is reused.

4 Transportation: The pallets used for transportation within Europe are returned for reuse.

5 Install: The tiles are supplied in recycled paper packaging, which can be recycled.

6 Maintain: Ceramic tiles are long-lasting, retaining their performance and appearance for many hundreds of years. Besides, individual tiles can be replaced should they become damaged.

7 Demolish and dispose of: The tiles are reusable and recyclable, and the company has begun a pilot project in the Netherlands collecting tile waste from construction sites for recycling into new tiles.

STEP BY STEP CARPET LIFE CYCLE

A number of carpet manufacturers are taking measures to address the environmental impact of their production processes. We explain below how InterfaceFLOR is mitigating its impact throughout the product life cycle of its carpet tiles.

1 Obtain: The manufacturer is focusing on sourcing local raw materials, and replacing petroleum-based yarn with recycled or renewable natural yarns. It uses bitumen-based carpet backing with a high recycled content.

2 Process: The company assesses its suppliers' sustainability credentials against its supply chain policy, and works with them to improve their environmental performance.

3 Manufacture: Energy-efficiency measures within the factories include intelligent conveyor systems and precision machinery to optimize water use and avoid waste. Its European factories run on renewable electricity and recycle postindustrial waste into new tiles.

4 Transportation: The manufacturer makes almost all the tiles it sells in Europe within Europe to limit delivery miles. Further, it is supporting its freight suppliers to reduce their environmental impact.

5 Install: The bitumen-based backing has low-VOC emissions and can be installed with a glueless adhesive system, promoting good air quality. Each of the company's biomimicry-inspired tiles is unique in appearance, creating a random, nondirectional floor pattern that minimizes waste. Customers can also opt into a carbon-offsetting project to compensate for their carpet's life cycle carbon emissions.

6 Maintain: The random floor pattern of the biomimicry-inspired tiles allows individual tiles to be replaced if they become worn or damaged, minimizing waste.

7 Demolish and dispose of: The company's recycling system means that postconsumer carpet tiles are collected at the end of their life, either for reuse or for recycling into new tiles or other products. The bitumen-based backing and solid adhesive are also recyclable, and the company is planning to introduce recycling of used yarn.

Approaching sustainable specification

It is apparent that we need to reduce our consumption of materials and choose them wisely to mitigate their environmental impact. Comparing the pros and cons of different materials can be bewildering. The familiar environmentalists' mantra of the three Rs—reduce, reuse, recycle—is helpful here. But we should add an extra R, for using renewables, when it comes to specifying building materials. To mitigate the environmental damage associated with materials, the interior designer's priorities must be to first reduce, second reuse, and third recycle, while ensuring that any new materials used are renewable. To fully understand whether a material is a sustainable choice, interior designers must consider its environmental impacts at every stage of its life cycle. As well as embodied energy and water, these might include pollution, habitat destruction, waste, and health issues. Each of the four Rs can be considered with reference to the life cycle.

Such rigor can help designers navigate "greenwash," where manufacturers emphasize an environmentally friendly aspect of their product, regardless of a less favorable full picture. Naturally, this sales technique is to be expected, so designers should be guided by independent sources and their own knowledge when finalizing their product choices. For example, an aluminum manufacturer may justly brag that its product is recyclable, but is unlikely to advertise the fact that it has very high embodied energy. That is not to say that aluminum is always an unsustainable choice—particularly as recycled aluminum has significantly lower embodied energy than virgin aluminum—simply that the energy used in its manufacture must be evaluated alongside its benefits.

As well as considering materials in isolation, we must consider how they are finished. Finishes, such as paints and varnishes, can have far greater environmental impact than the base material they are applied to, turning a benign material into an environmentally damaging component.

Interior designers are usually responsible for selecting all internal materials and finishes, so they are best placed to control the associated environmental impacts. Rather than being a negative constraint, sustainable specification offers vast scope for creativity.

As usual, the project type, location, and budget will guide the designer's decisions. Renovation projects may bring opportunities to creatively reuse existing materials, while new-build offers the chance to pioneer innovative, environmentally sound materials. The site location will dictate the materials, products, and skills that are locally available and therefore have relatively low embodied energy.

As with all environmental considerations, the project's intended duration will partly govern which materials are suitable. Thinking about what happens after demolition is paramount for temporary projects, so it is especially important to select reusable or recyclable materials. It is hard to justify using materials that have high embodied energy or significant impact on depleting resources for short-term projects, as any other benefits will not be enjoyed for long. Equally, materials should be used sparingly for maximum efficiency and perhaps prefabricated to lessen waste. Maintenance and durability will be of limited concern in shorter-term projects. Renewable, natural materials, efficiently used and put together simply, are likely to be the best option.

For flexible projects, materials or products serving more than one function would be ideal. Durable, low-maintenance materials will be essential to withstand wear and tear from frequent rearrangement.

On longer-term projects, the interior designer may be able to justify including some materials with higher embodied energy, particularly if they offer enhanced durability or thermal performance. These include high-technology materials that require more processing than their natural counterparts. As an example, despite its high embodied energy, synthetic insulation could be used to line a wall or roof to improve its thermal performance. As some synthetic insulation products offer high performance with thin layers, this could be the only way to reduce heat loss in an existing building, where space may be limited. Likewise, concrete, which has high embodied energy, could be used beneficially to provide exposed thermal mass, contributing to a passive solar design strategy. The durability and performance of materials are critical for long-term projects. Designers should consider the frequency and method of cleaning and maintenance that will be required over the lifetime of each product, as this might require water, chemicals, and energy. Air quality during occupation is a major concern, as the interior will be occupied, and influencing its occupants' health, for years to come.

STEP BY STEP SUSTAINABLE MATERIALS SPECIFICATION

When specifying sustainable materials the interior designer should first consider reducing, then reusing, then recycling, and, finally, using renewable sources. We see below how this approach can be applied to choosing flooring:

1 The first priority is to reduce the amount of materials used. This concrete floor, which has been finished to a high standard, avoids the need for a floor covering altogether.

2 The next best thing is to reuse materials, as shown by this reclaimed wood floor.

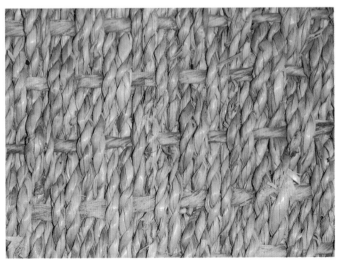

3 When new materials are needed, the best option is to use those with recycled content, such as this recycled rubber flooring.

4 If virgin materials cannot be avoided, it is important to choose those from renewable sources, such as this seagrass carpet.

Specification checklist

It is helpful to use a specification checklist to ensure you are considering all the environmental impacts associated with a material throughout its life cycle. The designer should aim to be able to answer yes to most of the questions on the following list:

Is the material needed?

Is it reused or reclaimed?

Is it sourced and processed near the site?

Is it from a renewable source?

Does it have low embodied energy and water?

Does its production have low environmental impact?

Does it have recycled content?

Does it have minimal or recyclable packaging?

Is it nontoxic and low-emitting during installation and use?

Does it improve the building's performance?

Do its application, treatment, and finishes have low environmental impact?

Does it require little maintenance or cleaning, and by nontoxic methods?

Can it be reused or recycled at the end of the project?

Reduce

The interior designer should begin by seeking to reduce the materials used in a project and their negative effects on the environment. This means reducing the amount of raw materials, as well as the waste, packaging, embodied energy and water, transportation, and air pollution associated with the materials used. A potential product's whole life cycle should be taken into account, so these environmental impacts can be reduced at every stage.

Reducing material use can be achieved on a fundamental level by questioning whether certain materials or products are needed at all. Supposing they are required, using materials that are untreated or self-finished, perhaps plywood or exposed brickwork, avoids the need for added finishes such as varnish, paint, or plaster. Using materials efficiently is another valid approach: metal could be used as a wide mesh rather than a solid sheet, and wood could be used as a thin veneer to cover a surface using minimal material. Similarly, products can be used efficiently by serving more than one function: say, a cork wall covering that also forms a tack board.

Ensuring that materials are hard-wearing and seldom require maintenance reduces the need for extra materials and minimizes waste once the space is in use. Durable materials are less likely to need to be repaired, refinished, or thrown away and replaced. And natural, biodegradable materials avoid creating a long-term landfill problem.

An important area that designers rarely consider is packaging, yet the materials we use to wrap products themselves contribute to waste and use finite resources.

Choosing products that require little protective packaging, and favoring suppliers that commit to limiting packaging or offer recycling systems for their packaging are both sensible approaches.

Evidently, selecting materials with low embodied energy and water reduces energy and water use. Choosing natural materials over man-made ones usually implies lower energy and water use during production, but there are noteworthy exceptions. The Sustainable Energy Research Team at Bath University in the UK offers a useful database of the embodied energy and carbon of common building materials.

LINK **www.bath.ac.uk/mech-eng/sert/embodied**

It is important to consider the environmental impact of the packaging a product comes in, as well as that of the product itself. Wrapping a material in excessive plastic packaging magnifies its ecological footprint.

Key

1   Earth blocks
2   Wood pellets
3   Oak frames
4   Roof slates
5   Sedum roof planting
6   Oak cladding
7   Lime plaster
8   Slate floor
9   Solar water heater
10 Wood insulation
11 Softwood studs and joists
12 Recycled aggregate and crushed brick
13 Low-E glass
14 Cellulose fiber insulation

A map like this can be used to chart the distances that sourced materials must travel to reach the site.

Interior designers can reduce the transportation emissions associated with their projects by using locally available materials and products. This avoids escalating the embodied energy that a product acquires after it leaves its source or the factory gates. The best options will vary widely between countries and sites, but using a local stone or wood species may be appropriate. On any site, earth blocks formed from soil excavated during construction can be used to form walls and are as local as a material can get. Using lightweight materials is also advantageous, as they require less fuel to transport them than heavier loads.

The final aspect to reduce is air pollution, during construction, occupation, and demolition. Chemicals used in finishes, treatments, binders, adhesives, and sealants are the main sources of VOC emissions. These can be contained in bound wood products, carpets, furniture, fabrics, paints, and varnishes. Seeking formaldehyde-free, low-VOC, or low-emitting products, and favoring natural materials and finishes, will help to engender good indoor air quality. Low-VOC finishes are also much pleasanter to apply, as they do not produce noxious fumes. Using organic versions of plant-based materials—such as cotton, wool, and hemp—means that chemical pesticides and fertilizers are avoided during cultivation. Synthetic dyes contribute to pollution during manufacture, so undyed or naturally dyed fabrics are a more environmentally friendly alternative. Finally, using dark or patterned materials will reduce the need for cleaning with products containing chemicals once the interior is in use. GreenGuard's website includes a database of low-emitting products, while the Green Product Innovation Institute catalogs nontoxic products.

LINK **www.greenguard.org; www.gpinnovation.org**

Reuse

Once the amount of materials used on a project and their associated impacts have been minimized, the next aim for the interior designer is to reuse materials. Again, this approach should be applied to the whole life cycle of a material. Reusing materials includes salvaging demolition waste, using reclaimed materials, and ensuring that specified materials can be reused at the end of the project. Reusing prevents existing materials going to waste in landfill and saves on the embodied energy and water that would have been necessary to produce replacement materials. In practice, reusing is often inextricably linked to reducing, as using existing materials can reduce the need for new ones. Reusing avoids the need for many virgin raw materials and all the environmental problems they cause throughout their life cycle.

If it is not practical to retain an existing building, materials can be salvaged during demolition for reuse in its successor. Bricks, doors, and cabinetry are good examples. The same applies to renovation projects, as serviceable elements of the existing interior can be retained for reuse in the new project. Carpet tiles, light fixtures, drapes, and furniture may all be suitable. In any case, the interior designer should consider the outcome of any demolition that happens to enable their project. If the existing materials cannot be reused in the project, can they be recycled, donated to local salvage yards or flea markets, given to charities, or advertised for sale?

Vintage products include inventive designs, such as this chair by Reestore made from a reclaimed supermarket cart.

Reclaimed materials can also be sourced from other projects, typically through salvage yards, flea markets antiques stores, or vintage suppliers. This is an excellent way to find unique, characterful products to set your design apart, and the cost is often lower than buying anew. Limitless items are available but could include fabrics, furniture, fixtures, wooden flooring, and bricks. Materials need not be reused in the way that was originally intended, but could be repurposed, giving enormous scope for creativity. For instance, drapes could be revived to upholster a chair, or a rug could be reinvented as a wall hanging. Some product designers specialize in making repurposed objects, from light fixtures to furniture. Websites like Salvo provide directories of available and wanted salvaged building materials.

LINK **www.salvoweb.com**

Finally, it is vital to consider whether the materials you specify could be reused in another project at the end of your project's life. Products made to standard sizes in classic colors will be easier to incorporate into another design.

Recycle

Recycling materials is the next priority. Recycling is distinct from reusing in that existing materials are reprocessed into a new form. It diverts waste materials from landfill and reduces the amount of virgin resources needed to make new products. Reusing is more effective than recycling because of the extra energy, water, and transportation needed for the recycling process. To promote recycling, an interior designer can choose recycled-content products, provide facilities for recycling when the space is in use and ensure that the materials they specify can be recycled at the end of the project's life.

Here Reestore has turned a salvaged bath into a unique chaise longue.

A wide range of recycled-content products is available to the interior designer, from basic background materials such as particle board, gypsum wall board, and carpet underlay, to more glamorous finishing materials such as glass, carpets, plastic sheeting, fabric ceilings, rubber flooring, and ceramic tiles.

An easy but important design measure is to provide storage space for recycling once the interior is occupied. Specifying recycling bins for different types of recyclable waste and ensuring these are conveniently sited in the layout will encourage the building's users to recycle. If the project has some outdoor space, or access to organic waste collections, composting bins can also be provided for recycling food waste.

Interior designers should check the materials they select are recyclable, noting that, while many materials are theoretically recyclable, local recycling systems will determine which products can be recycled in practice. Plastic recycling in particular can be problematic, as each of the many plastic types must be recycled separately. The best scenario is to choose a product covered by a manufacturer recycling system, which is becoming common for carpets. Simple products made of single materials will be easier to isolate for recycling than composite products made of several materials fused together. Finishing is also important, as painting or varnishing a material like wood may mean it will not be accepted by a recycling system. The Waste Resources Action Programme (WRAP) and Rematerialise websites include databases of recycled-content materials.

LINK **www.wrap.org.uk;**
rcproducts.wrap.org.uk;
extranet.kingston.ac.uk/rematerialise

Renewables

When using virgin materials is unavoidable, interior designers must take care to specify ones that originate from renewable sources. This is valid for both natural and synthetic materials, as synthetic materials rely on natural ingredients.

For natural materials, designers should seek plentiful, fast-growing, and self-replenishing materials. Abundant tree species include ash and larch. Bamboo and hemp are fast-growing plants. Animal products, such as sheep's wool and alpaca, are self-replenishing, while cork oak trees can be repeatedly harvested. Designers should avoid potential causes of illegal forest clearance, such as uncertified rubber, and wood from poorly regulated countries and scarce species. The best way is to insist that wood and rubber come from a certified renewable source. Greenpeace's and Friends of the Earth's Good Wood Guides rank tree species according to their vulnerability.

LINK **www.greenpeace.org.uk; www.foe.co.uk**

With man-made materials, we need to be aware of the raw ingredients and their environmental impacts: for instance, plastics derive from finite fossil fuels and concrete may use gravel dredged from marine habitats. Recycled plastics and concrete made from recycled aggregates are much better options.

"The best friend on earth of man is the tree. When we use the tree respectfully and economically, we have one of the greatest resources on the earth." FRANK LLOYD WRIGHT

Far left
Recycled-content materials available to the interior designer include recycled glass wall tiles.

Left
Cork is a self-replenishing material and therefore a renewable resource.

Case study Choosing materials

Molo's Innovation/Imagination exhibit at the Milan Furniture Fair (Italy) showcased the company's innovative products. Their Soft range of furniture, lighting, and screens uses materials with low environmental impact and construction that supports flexible living.

The products are made from a simple palette of materials, consisting of Kraft paper or textiles, with concealed LED lighting or bamboo charcoal dye added to create variations. The stiff paper, which is unbleached and 50% recycled, is robust and recyclable at the end of its life. Used for both the seating and screens, it can be left a natural brown or dyed black. The textile, made of polyethylene, is also recyclable and has up to 15% recycled content. The translucent white fabric is used for the lighting, seating, and screens. It can be lit up by internal low-energy LEDs or, for the screens and seating, dyed black.

The construction of each product is driven by the desire to enable flexibility. The products are lightweight and portable, allowing occupants to install and rearrange them as desired, while their cellular structure ensures they are strong enough to withstand this. The construction is modular to enable the products to be fixed together in different combinations. The Softwall and Softblock screens are freestanding and their components can be joined together to suit the required height, length, and shape. Softseating has magnetic ends that can be joined together to form a cylindrical stool or coffee table, or connected to other pieces to create long, linear benches. The Cloud Softlight comes in three sizes that can be hung as individual pendants or in various combinations to fill the space.

Opposite
The individual components can be used to make cylindrical stools. The seating is also available in black, dyed with bamboo charcoal, or in textile.

Below
The exhibition showcases the Soft range of flexible screens, lighting, and furniture, made of a simple palette of sustainable materials.

Above
This lightweight seating made of unbleached, recycled-content Kraft paper is easy to install and rearrange. Here many modules are being joined together to form benches.

Below
This recycled-content textile version of the modular screen contains low-energy LED lighting. The lightweight, cellular structure is freestanding and its modular components can be joined together to make screens of different heights and lengths. The screens also come in brown or dyed-black paper.

Below
These lights are hollow spheres of translucent white textile with internal low-energy LEDs. They can be used as individual pendants or combined in multiples to fill an interior.

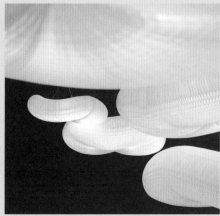

TIP BEWARE GREENWASH

Watch out for unscrupulous manufacturers who try to make their products seem greener than they actually are. Be guided instead by independent sources of information and assessment, and learn how to spot a sustainable product for yourself.

Materials assessment

Materials can be evaluated as part of a whole-design assessment, as described in Chapter 2. It is also useful to assess materials in isolation, either to support a whole-design assessment or in place of one. Obtaining formal certification of materials can help the interior designer objectively evaluate their environmental credentials and substantiate them to the client. Some assessments analyze all environmental aspects of a material, while others focus on a particular aspect, such as organic production, responsible sourcing, or air quality. Certified products will carry an official logo and come together with certification documents.

Many organizations offer systems that consider all environmental impacts of a product. Examples include BioRegional and WWF's One Planet Living system, which has a global emphasis; MBDC's Cradle to Cradle and EcoLogo in North America; Environmental Choice in New Zealand; and Green Mark in Asia. One Planet Living considers ten principles for sustainable living—carbon, waste, transportation, materials, food, water, wildlife, culture, equity, and health—and approves products that are exemplary in these areas.

LINK **www.oneplanetliving.org; www.mbdc.com**

Other companies, such as the Building Research Establishment (BRE) in the UK and Athena Institute (Athena SMI) in North America, assess the environmental impacts of generic materials throughout their life cycle. BRE's Green Guide to Specification, which includes sections on floor finishes and internal partitions, gives an environmental rating for different options. Under flooring ceramic mosaic tiles have a rating of A+, representing best practice, while terrazzo is E-rated. Athena SMI's EcoCalculator for Assemblies is an equivalent tool, which also covers internal walls and floors.

LINK **www.thegreenguide.org.uk; www.athenasmi.org**

Several systems certify organic production of textiles, including the Soil Association Organic Standard in Europe, Oregan Tilth in North America, and, worldwide, the Better Cotton Initiative (BCI) and the Global Organic Textile Standard.

LINK **www.soilassociation.org**

A number of organizations monitor responsible sourcing of wood and rubber, providing chain of custody certification confirming that the wood is from a sustainably managed forest. The best known are the global Forest Stewardship Council (FSC) and Programme for the Endorsement of Forest Certification (PEFC). Others include the Rainforest Alliance and Sustainable Forestry Initiative in North America; and the Australian Forest Stewardship Scheme.

LINK **www.fsc.org**

Products that do not impair indoor air quality are certified by GreenGuard in North America; Eurofins Indoor Air Comfort and Eco-Institut in Europe; and SCS Indoor Advantage worldwide.

Recycled-content products can be identified by the ubiquitous generic recycled symbol, which should not be confused with the various recyclable symbols.

The Green Dot is a recycling system for recycling packaging. It originated in Germany and now covers 26 countries.

LINK **www.gruener-punkt.de**

Suppliers can gain accreditation for themselves, as well as their products, in recognition of operation methods and production processes that consider the environment. Interior designers can look out for environmentally accredited manufacturers for reassurance that they monitor and continually improve their environmental performance, and are independently audited. The principal standards are the European Management and Audit Scheme (EMAS) and the internationally recognized ISO 14001.

Right
This symbol is found on recycled products.

Below
Wood arrives on site bearing the Forest Stewardship Council (FSC) stamp, "the mark of responsible forestry," showing it comes from a sustainable source.

TIP CERTIFIED MATERIALS

Seek materials and suppliers that are independently certified for their environmental performance. Details of materials certification systems worldwide can be found on the Global Ecolabelling Network's website:

www.ecolabelling.org

Choosing materials

We have learned that there is plenty for the interior designer to consider when choosing sustainable materials, but that many independent resources are available to assist. We will now look at how to apply this knowledge to compare the environmental impact of different materials for each element of the interior. We will cover the main issues to consider when specifying base materials, flooring, finishes, fabrics, and furniture. We will also recommend additional useful online product databases and guidance for further information.

While tried-and-tested natural materials and traditional building techniques undoubtedly have their place in environmentally conscious design, the interior designer should also be open to newer materials and construction methods. Recent developments, such as nanotechnology, digital imagery, biomimicry, and LEDs, are producing "smart" materials that can bring environmental benefits in energy saving and performance. Innovations range from illuminated wallpaper to thermally insulating paint. Transmaterial, Materia, and Mutant Materials are useful databases of innovative materials.

LINK www.transmaterial.net; www.materia.nl; www.mutantmaterials.com

Base materials

Base materials that often form part of the interior designer's repertoire are wooden boards, glass, metals, and gypsum wall board. These may form a finished surface or provide a base for finishing materials.

Wooden boards Wooden boards include particle boards, plywoods, cement boards, and fiberboards. On the one hand, these boards make efficient use of wood, using minimal quantities to make lightweight, strong boards in large panel sizes. On the other hand, they often include toxic resins and wood from nonrenewable sources.

Fiberboards, such as medium-density fiberboard (MDF), consist of bonded softwood dust. Despite being an effective use of waste from wood processing, the wood is usually bound with toxic resins that add to internal air pollution. The designer should seek boards with formaldehyde-free resins and check that the wood is from waste or certified sources. Strawboard, which recycles waste agricultural straw and has low embodied energy if locally sourced, is another good option.

Particle boards, such as oriented strand board (OSB), are made by bonding chips of wood with resin. They have high embodied energy, needing heat in their production, and use toxic formaldehyde-based resins. Versions using recycled and certified wood, however, how lessen the environmental burden.

Plywood consists of thin sheets of wood glued together for combined strength. Again, it has high embodied energy and often uses toxic formaldehyde resins, and it is important to check that it contains certified wood.

Cement board is made up of reinforcing fibers bound with cement. The cement gives it high embodied energy and means the product is defined as hazardous waste, but some boards contain recycled waste wood.

Fiberboards are the most environmentally sound wood board, but for all boards interior designers should insist on formaldehyde-free resins and certified wood.

Glass Glass has medium embodied energy and is made from natural, plentiful resources. It is nontoxic and can be recycled. Recycled glass products, such as tiles and counter-tops, are available and reduce embodied energy and waste.

Metals Metals have much higher embodied energy than glass—stratospheric in the case of virgin aluminum—and depend on nonrenewable resources. Nevertheless, recycled metals are available, which reduce embodied energy and conserve raw materials. The manufacturing process is extremely polluting, but the end product is hard-wearing and nontoxic. Beware of finishing metals with chrome plating, as its manufacture exploits scarce natural resources and generates toxic waste.

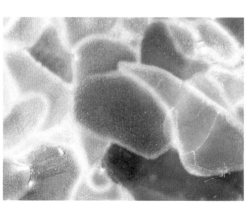

Far left
When specifying plywood, look for certified wood and formaldehyde-free resins.

Left
Recycled glass tiles, countertops, and wall surfaces are widely available.

Drywall Drywall is made of gypsum. It has low embodied energy and can contribute to thermal insulation. Nevertheless, it is responsible for significant waste, both during installation and at the end of its life, and contains polluting sulfates. Recycled-content gypsum wall board is available and helps divert waste gypsum from landfill.

Flooring

When choosing a floor surface, an interior designer has numerous natural and synthetic options. Natural coverings include hard finishes such as wood, bamboo, and ceramic or stone tiles; smooth, soft finishes such as cork, linoleum, and rubber; and carpets made of wool, cotton, or plant fibers such as seagrass, sisal, coir, and hessian. Man-made alternatives comprise smooth finishes such as recycled rubber; vinyl; and carpets made from recycled PET, nylon, polypropylene, and polyester.

On the one hand, hard finishes are highly durable and recyclable, but on the other they can have high embodied energy, as is the case with stone transported from faraway countries. Locally sourced wood has low embodied energy, yet it is vital to ensure a renewable source by choosing an abundant species from a well-managed forest. With wood laminate floors, designers should check that the woods used for both the veneer and its backing are sustainably sourced. As mentioned previously, bamboo is extremely renewable as it is a fast-growing plant, yet it will have high embodied energy if used on a project remote from Asia and it is important to check that the source does not threaten panda habitat.

Natural soft materials tend to be renewable, biodegradable, nontoxic, and durable, but pollution from fertilizers used in their production and the embodied energy associated with importing them should be taken into account. For example, the fertilizer used to grow linseed to make linoleum causes water and air pollution, while sourcing cork from overseas increases its embodied energy. Nevertheless, the synthetic alternative of vinyl is a greater evil: although similarly durable, it relies on finite fossil fuels for its raw materials and degrades extremely slowly in landfill.

Waste is a key consideration with carpets, which are responsible for significant amounts of waste during manufacture and after use. However, recycled-content carpets are available and some manufacturers offer recycling systems to address the problem. Natural fibers have low embodied energy if sourced locally and derive from renewable sources, but can produce toxic waste during their growth and treatment. To produce wool, toxic chemicals are used in sheep dipping, while growing cotton is associated with intensive use of pesticides. In addition, most carpets need regular cleaning after installation, using water, energy, and chemical products.

The most sustainable floor materials include cork, linoleum, local stone, wool, plant fibers, and certified or reclaimed wood. Vinyl and nonrecycled nylon should generally be avoided.

Where an underlay is needed, for example with carpets, a natural material, such as felt or hessian, or a recycled one, such as recycled rubber, is the best choice.

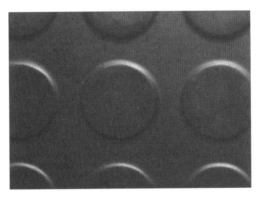

Far left
Wood veneers are available from renewable sources.

Left
Choose rubber flooring from a certified sustainable source.

Far left
Seek recycled-content carpets and underlays whose manufacturers offer end-of-life recycling systems.

Left
Cork is a sustainable choice for flooring, being a renewable material and providing a durable finish.

Care should be taken to avoid sealants with high VOC emissions for use with, say, cork, stone, or wood. The Sustainable Floors website offers guidance on the environmental impact of flooring.

LINK **www.sustainablefloors.co.uk**

Finishes

Possible finishes include paints, sealants, plasters, and wallpapers. These can be used on many surfaces, from walls, floors, and ceilings to furniture and fixtures. Mineral paint, clay paint, oil-based emulsion, water- or acrylic-borne plant-based paint, cassein, and limewash are natural paints; man-made alternatives comprise vinyl or acrylic emulsion, and water- or solvent-borne synthetic paint. Natural wallpaper can be made of paper, plant fiber, silk, or cotton, while vinyl and foil are synthetic options. Sealants include natural hard waxes, linseed oil, and tung oil, and manufactured water- or solvent-borne varnishes. Plaster is made from clay, lime, gypsum, or cement.

Paints Paint consists of a solvent, binder, and pigment, all of which have environmental impacts. They are termed water-based (acrylic) or solvent-based (oil), depending on the solvent used. Paints emit VOCs from solvents during application and once the interior is in use. Synthetic paints create much higher concentrations of VOCs, particularly those that are solvent-based. Synthetic paints are also responsible for high amounts of hazardous waste during their production and disposal, and use nonrenewable petroleum. Natural paints are less toxic but also less durable. Ecoartisan's website gives guidance on natural paints.

LINK **wwww.ecoartisan.org**

Sealants Sealants are used to protect and color wood. Varnishes emit toxic fumes when applied, but are stable once set. Water-based varnishes with lower emissions are available. Oils tend to contain drying additives and produce toxic emissions for weeks after application. Waxes, although based on natural ingredients, typically contain harmful additives, including formaldehyde. But all-natural products, which combine beeswax and carnauba wax with natural oils and resins, are available. When using stains, nontoxic, water-based products colored with natural pigments are best.

Plasters Embodied energy and waste are primary considerations when comparing plasters. In terms of embodied energy, cement has the highest, gypsum and lime follow, and clay has the lowest. Cement has the added problem of being nonrecyclable, while gypsum and lime are hazardous if they end up in landfill. Natural clay plasters are nontoxic, renewable, and recyclable providing they do not contain synthetic additives.

Wallpapers Natural wallpapers use renewable materials, whereas vinyl and foil use finite resources, cause pollution, and create disposal problems; vinyl is also known for off-gassing. However, nonorganic cotton should be avoided and paper should be from a sustainable wood source. The adhesives used to apply wallpaper may be the biggest concern, as they can be toxic. The interior designer should specify water-based glue and lightweight wallpaper to avoid the need for stronger adhesives.

In summary, it is prudent to avoid man-made paints, ideally opting instead for linseed oil-based emulsion with natural pigments or water-borne plant-based paint. If sealing is essential, water-based varnish, natural oil without additives, and beeswax made with natural resins are the best products. For wall coverings, natural wallpaper, such as certified or recycled paper, and clay plaster are ideal.

Far left
When using paints, opt for natural versions.

Left
Environmentally conscious wallpaper options include VOC-free products printed on sustainably sourced paper.

Organic cotton is a good choice for fabrics, as it requires less water in its production than traditional cotton and avoids toxic pesticides.

Fabrics

The interior designer can chose from an array of fabrics, whether for drapes, blinds, wall coverings, furniture upholstery, or cushions. Natural materials include wool, cotton, felt, hemp, hessian, and leather; while nylon, polyester, acrylic, acetate and rayon, and polypropylene are the synthetic choices.

Fabrics are linked to many environmental issues in their production and maintenance. Unfortunately, the choice between natural and man-made fabrics is by no means clear-cut here. As usual, the man-made materials require high amounts of energy and water during their manufacture, but the manufacturing process is largely nonpolluting. Conversely, dyeing and treating natural fibers causes significant water pollution; and emissions from cleaning and transporting the raw materials must be considered. In particular, cotton production uses vast amounts of water and pesticides, and requires intensive treatment using hazardous chemicals. Organic cotton, which avoids harmful pesticides and uses less water, is far better—as are alternative fabrics such as hessian, made from hardier hemp or jute plants.

The natural materials are all renewable, whereas their synthetic counterparts often use finite resources. Nylon, polyester, acrylic, and polypropylene are petroleum-based and therefore use fossil fuels. But acetate and rayon are man-made from renewable natural fibers.

Synthetic fabrics are nonbiodegradable, contributing to long-term waste. Leather avoids waste, as it is a by-product of meat, but designers should check that its source guarantees high standards of animal welfare. In addition, leather is to blame for pollution, as toxic chemicals are used in the tanning and dyeing processes, as well as for cleaning during maintenance. Suede and chamois in particular require frequent cleaning. Products formed from waste from the leather industry overcome some of these issues.

On balance, natural fabrics such as wool, felt, and hessian seem the sensible choice, providing the designer checks their origin and sources products that mitigate adverse environmental effects through their production methods. As with flooring, it is wise to avoid vinyl, nonrecycled nylon, and nonorganic cotton. It is imperative to seek fabrics that are either undyed or colored with natural dyes, although the latter still cause some pollution. Another trick is to use dark or patterned fabrics, on which dirt and stains will be less obvious, reducing the frequency of cleaning needed once they are in use.

Furniture

Furniture can be made of wood, bamboo, cardboard, metal, plastics, and fabrics. Many of these materials have already been discussed above and the same issues apply. In addition, it is worth noting that cardboard can be a sustainable option where durability is not a major concern, but certified and recycled sources should be sought. Plastics, as explained for types like vinyl above, use non-renewable petroleum, require a polluting manufacturing process, emit toxic chemicals, and create long-term waste. Recycled plastics address some of these issues.

Local certified wood or cardboard are perhaps the best materials to choose, in conjunction with the fabrics recommended above, for new furniture. But the potential of using reclaimed furniture, which is widely available from antiques stores and easy to fit into any interior project, should not be discounted. Vintage finds can include chairs, tables, sofas, and beds, as well as accessories from lamps to pictures to sculptural objects.

Further information

There are a host of useful online databases to help interior designers source sustainable products. Some of these databases catalog generic sustainable building materials, while others focus on certain characteristics, such as recycled content. We have already mentioned in this section Materia, Transmaterial, and Mutant Materials for innovative products; Rematerialise and WRAP for recycled-content products; and GreenGuard and Green Product Innovation Institute for low-emitting products. In addition, One Planet Products, Selector's Sustainable Products section, Green Industry Resource, Green Building Source (Oikos), and Greenspec's Green Building Products section provide classified directories of sustainable products. These independent sources are most likely to be impartial, but specialist stockists of sustainable construction products are also useful sources of information.

Inventive reclaimed furnishings can add interest to an interior. These lamps by Guy Trench of Antiques by Design are made from old Second World War helmets.

TIP MATERIALS DATABASES

Consult databases of sustainable materials to source products with low environmental impact:

selector.com/au/sustainable
www.greenspec.co.uk
www.oneplanetproducts.com
www.greenindustryresource.com
www.greenbuildingstore.co.uk
www.oikos.com

Construction methods

As well as considering materials and finishes in isolation, we must take into account how they are assembled. The choice of construction methods will affect a project's environmental impact, and interior designers are in a strong position to influence this. We will now look at the significance of construction methods in environmentally conscious design and how to select sustainable building techniques, for both whole interiors and individual components such as furniture.

Impacts of construction methods

The way materials are combined and fixed together can contribute to climate change, resource depletion, waste, health issues, and water scarcity.

Construction methods can determine an interior's thermal performance and maintenance requirements, affecting energy use and thus climate change. Combining different materials in different thicknesses affects thermal performance, which is critical for passive control of energy use, as we saw in the energy section. The nature and frequency of maintenance affects embodied energy, as discussed in the materials section. Much energy is used to power tools and equipment on building sites: construction methods that require cranes for a long period will be especially energy-intensive.

Certain construction methods, such as solid brick or block partitions, can be very wasteful of resources, relying on a significant quantity of material to form a sturdy component. Similarly, construction details, such as joints and junctions between materials, that are very elaborate may use more material than is strictly necessary for the purpose. In addition, construction that does not work with the strengths of the materials used will prevent an economical use of resources. Using more weight of material than needed also affects vehicular emissions, since extra fuel will be required to transport the materials from source to site.

Building methods have a significant effect on the amount of waste that is produced during construction, during the operation of the interior, and once the interior is demolished. Poorly thought-out construction that does not take account of standard modules and requires many products to be cut to fit on site leads to the offcuts being wasted. Equally, designs that do not acknowledge minimum orders and batch sizes of products may necessitate over-ordering, with the excess material simply going to waste. Materials that need to be ordered in advance are vulnerable to becoming damaged by the weather or broken when they are stored on site, resulting in waste.

Carr's Country Victoria House in Kilmore (Australia) is built using a prefabricated, modular system. It is designed as a series of interconnected pavilions to suit the standard modules, which allow quick construction and flexibility of layout.

Construction methods have an ongoing influence on waste once the interior is complete. If the construction is not sufficiently robust for its purpose, components will quickly become damaged in use and need to be repaired or replaced. The rejected components will end up in landfill, unless they can be recycled. Moreover, once the whole interior is no longer needed, if the construction methods fuse materials together, they cannot be easily separated for reuse or recycling.

Products such as adhesives and sealants often used to fix materials together can contain VOCs that harm human health. These may affect construction workers, as emissions are likely to be at their highest levels during application, as well as occupants, either when an existing interior is being upgraded while still occupied or when emissions continue once an interior is complete.

Significant amounts of water are used on construction sites, contributing to water scarcity. Traditional, wet construction methods, such as brick laying, plastering, and cement mixing, use the most water.

Approaching sustainable construction

It follows that the prime considerations for achieving sustainable construction are enhancing thermal performance and minimizing energy use on site, using materials effectively, designing out waste, promoting health, and limiting water use on site. As materials and construction methods go hand in hand, we can again follow the "reduce, reuse, recycle" approach introduced in the materials section.

As with materials, interior designers should explore modern methods of construction (MMC), as well as traditional building techniques, as both can bring environmental benefits.

As always, the approach taken for construction should suit the project type. If the interior is required to last only a short time, it should be constructed with a view to deconstruction, avoiding bonding mixed materials, to aid reclamation and recycling after use. A good solution is to design simple slotted, screwed, or bolted joints and avoid adhesives. It will also be important to ensure ease of transportation, installation, and dismantling, using lightweight, flat-pack, and prefabricated constructions.

Flexible spaces might include reconfigurable furniture or shelving, movable partitions, or access panels to allow concealed systems to be changed. Robust construction will be needed to avoid damage from frequent modifications. Connectors may need to be capable of quick and simple adjustment to support adaptations.

Both flexible and long-term projects should still be constructed with their eventual demolition in mind. Long-term projects demand durable construction that is built to last, or components that can easily be replaced should they become damaged. Strong mechanical connectors can be used to enable dismantling, and should last longer than adhesives in any case. Traditional, solid construction methods may be justified, as their advantages will be enjoyed for a long time, perhaps outweighing the disadvantages of high energy and water use on site.

Opposite
Incubation, a flexible retail unit in Melbourne (Australia) by Matt Gibson Architecture + Design, includes adjustable flaps to allow the space to be quickly reconfigured.

Left
Long-term projects, such as Ripple Design's Courtyard House in Los Angeles (US), can afford to use materials with reasonably high embodied energy. Here, exposed concrete floors have been chosen for their durability, to enhance thermal mass, and to avoid the need for a separate floor finish; a steel structure was chosen over wood to avoid termite damage.

Reduce

Appropriate construction methods can help reduce the building industry's impact on raw materials, waste, energy and water use, and air pollution.

An interior's thermal performance can be maximized by using insulation or exposed thermal mass, as described in the energy section, reducing energy demand. Insulation can be applied to the interior face of external walls, floors, and roofs to improve the building fabric, and around hot-water systems to promote energy efficiency. To benefit from thermal mass, the interior designer can use unfinished solid surfaces, such as brick walls and concrete floors, in locations where they will absorb heat from the sun.

Insulation is perhaps an overlooked behind-the-scenes product, but the interior designer should make every effort to use it to enhance the thermal performance of the space. This is especially true in renovation projects, where lining the existing envelope with insulation can dramatically improve energy performance. Natural insulation materials include cork, sheep's wool, hemp, flax, reinforcing fibers,

Above
Sheep's wool is a natural option for insulation.

Right
Mihaly Slocombe's Hill House in Merricks (Australia) contains a rammed-earth wall to provide thermal mass.

and wood fiber; synthetic products include cellulose (recycled newspaper), rock mineral wool, and glass mineral wool; and expanded polystyrene, extruded polystyrene, and rigid polyurethane are fossil-fuel-based products.

Thermal performance should be the primary consideration on longer-term projects, where the energy-saving benefits of materials achieving lower u-values will be noticed for years. This may favor synthetic materials if space is limited, as natural insulation materials typically need to be thicker in order to achieve a comparable performance. Natural options tend to have lower embodied energy and are therefore particularly suited to shorter-term projects. Fossil-fuel-derived products should be avoided if possible, as they rely on nonrenewable resources. In addition, they release hydrocarbons in manufacture that contribute to ozone depletion. Seeking insulation products with an Ozone Depletion Potential (ODP) of zero and Global Warming Potential (GWP) of less than 5 is good practice.

Designing with efficient structures, such as cellular construction, can support the aim of using materials

The extension of Barrow House in Melbourne (Australia) by Andrew Maynard Architects achieves a solid appearance, despite using lightweight wood construction to economize on material, by thickening sections of the walls and ceilings. Components from the existing house, including the living room furniture, have been reused.

Above

Hollow steel modules were used for Koby Cottage in Albion (US) by Garrison Architects. The modules were prefabricated in a factory and arrived on site complete with interior fixtures.

Below

BaleHaus in Bath (UK) by White Design combines traditional and modern construction techniques. Its prefabricated wall panels are made of wood and straw.

sparingly to avoid wasting resources. For example, corrugated cardboard is inherently rigid, despite having a hollow core and thus using a limited amount of material. Assembling materials in an "honest" manner that capitalizes on and expresses their natural characteristics without distracting ornamentation is an efficient approach. Similarly, using lightweight construction for partitions, based on wooden or metal frameworks rather than solid materials, such as brick or blockwork, uses less material. Such lightweight construction methods also limit emissions from transportation.

Waste can also be reduced by choosing prefabricated construction methods, such as doorsets, staircases, bathroom and kitchen pods, and partitions with integral systems. Because these are assembled to precise dimensions under controlled factory conditions and delivered to site just in time for installation, waste from over-ordering, cutting to size, or damage during storage is avoided. Any waste material that is produced in the factory is usually put back into the manufacturing process. Repeated or standard elements are usually needed to justify the expense of prefabrication, hence further efficiencies can be achieved by reusing the same molds to form components.

Even with traditional, in-situ construction, designing to suit standard modules of products such as tiles and gypsum wall board avoids waste from leftovers and gives a neat finished appearance.

Ensuring that your design suits the occupants' needs, and incorporates flexibility and adaptability in case their needs change, can avoid the whole interior being replaced in future. As well as leaving a more lasting legacy, this avoids all the materials used in your project going to waste. For example, sliding or folding partitions could allow a school to transform its assembly hall into smaller teaching spaces, while reconfigurable displays could allow a retail unit's look to be quickly refreshed.

Avoiding or carefully specifying adhesives can enhance indoor air quality, reducing health problems. Adhesives are an admittedly unglamorous but usually ubiquitous element of the interior and must be considered as part of a sustainable design. Like paints, they are either solvent- or water-based; the water-based variants are less toxic during application and use. The best are PVA-based glue and water-soluble cassein. The interior designer should consider the adhesive needed when selecting surface materials, as a sustainable material becomes suddenly less so if it relies on a potent adhesive.

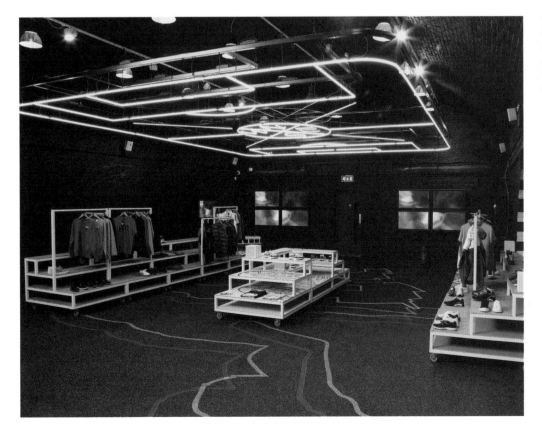

Wilson Brothers used modular display units within Nike East London 1948 (UK). The modules are on wheels and can be stacked in different ways, enabling considerable flexibility.

Reuse

Reusing construction can be as simple as keeping all or part of an existing building, as in a renovation project. Since interior designers often work within existing buildings they have many opportunities to revive interesting parts of buildings, and this can give the finished design its character. As discussed in the energy section, the retained building should ideally be upgraded to update its thermal performance and systems to modern best-practice standards. Waste can be avoided by reusing the basic construction—from elements of structure, to walls and floors, to carcasses of kitchen cabinets.

All these elements can be given new life by adding finishes, or even stripping back outdated coverings to reveal the original construction beyond.

Another possibility is to source reclaimed construction materials from salvage yards or through websites such as Salvo and Builder Scrap.

LINK **www.builderscrap.com**

Left
The existing brick walls and wooden roof structure were reused in Ryan Russell's H + B Fashion store in Victoria (Australia).

Above
At the Andels Manufaktura hotel in Lodz (Poland), Jestico + Whiles converted a former textile factory. The existing building's iron columns, brickwork walls, and vaulted brick ceilings bring character to the restaurant.

Assembly methods are critical to ensure the materials and components can be reused at the end of the project's life. Avoiding bonding materials at all, using slots, is the simplest method, but will not always provide adequate robustness. Alternatively, materials can be secured with removable mechanical connectors, including hooks, clamps, screws, and bolts, making them easier to dismantle intact for reuse than those that are fused together with adhesives or welds. Similarly, as nails are harder to remove than screws, they could render materials like wood impossible to reuse.

Recycle

As with reuse, the attachment method must be considered to ensure that materials can easily be dismantled into their component parts for recycling. The same principles, of using connections that can readily be undone, apply.

Jumbo Stay in Stockholm (Sweden) reuses a redundant Boeing 747 airplane to create an unusual hotel and museum.

Furniture construction

Looking at furniture is a good way to understand how to achieve sustainable construction, as furniture design demonstrates construction techniques on a small, manageable scale.

Rawstudio's hanging chair shows how simple volumes can easily be created using a lightweight sheet material, in this case plywood. The product is supplied flat-packed for ease of transportation and uses minimal material to create a three-dimensional form. The plywood rings are held

Below
Rawstudio's concept sketch for its hanging chair imagines how a three-dimensional chair will be made by threading a rope through flat plywood rings.

Above
The flat plywood components of the hanging chair.

Right
Rope threaded through the plywood rings creates a three-dimensional chair that hangs from the ceiling.

together by a rope, allowing them to be hung anywhere, indoors or outside, promoting flexibility.

Michael Marriott designed shelving that celebrated the beauty of simple construction and the possibilities of high-technology connectors for his XYZ exhibition. A die-cast metal connector was developed that enabled the wooden shelves to be easily constructed, reconfigured, and dismantled. The connectors are expressed and brightly colored to highlight their function. The shelves and uprights can be taken apart for reuse or recycling, by unscrewing the connectors, when no longer needed. The shelves are lightweight and can be flat-packed for transportation. Unlike typical freestanding shelves, they do not have a solid back, using as little material as possible.

We have seen in this chapter how interior designers can choose energy and water systems, materials, and construction methods with a view to tackling environmental issues. We have discovered that the secret to doing this successfully is to remember basic priorities, and to refer to independent guidance and assessment when making detailed choices.

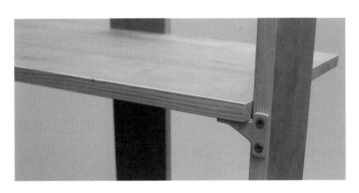

Above
Michael Marriott's shelving units for the XYZ exhibition are held together by die-cast metal connectors, enabling quick assembly and disassembly.

Right
The XYZ shelves use wood efficiently by using single planks to support the back and sides.

Case study Sustainable construction
Extensions by Aïssa Logerot

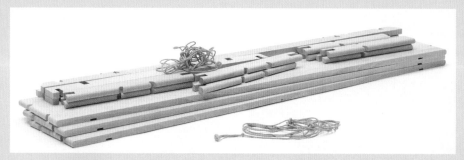

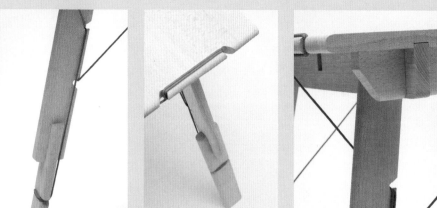

Left
The wood and string arrive on site as a flat-packed kit of parts.

Below left, middle, and right
The wooden components slot neatly together and are then bound tight by the string.

Bottom
The pieces form items of furniture, such as this desk, and include optional elements such as this task lamp that can be added on to suit the user's needs.

The Extensions range of furniture by Aïssa Logerot demonstrates a simple construction method that makes efficient use of materials, promotes flexible living, and allows for recycling. A set of wooden components is bound together with string to form a table or desk.

The string secures and braces the structure adequately, but can easily be unwound to allow the table to be dismantled for transporting elsewhere or recycling. The simple construction method means the kit of parts can be delivered flat and assembled by anyone. The string is vividly colored, making a design feature of the ingenious construction technique.

The range includes a selection of clip-on accessories, such as a lamp, allowing users to customize the desk to suit their needs.

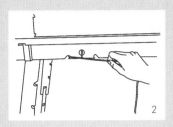
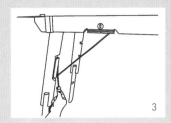

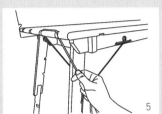
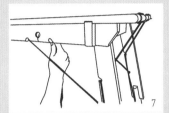

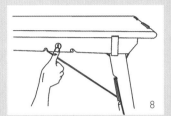

Above
An assembly guide for a table in this range explains the product's simple construction method. The flat-packed components are bound together with string.

Below
This Extensions shelving unit shows how the components come together.

Below
Elements were specially designed so that they could be slotted and tied together.

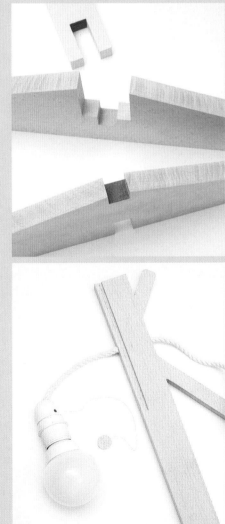

STEP BY STEP FLAT-PACK FURNITURE

Kapteinbolt's 90° Furniture range shows great use of a sheet material that can be delivered flat and then opened up to form a three-dimensional object. The aim of the product was to reduce the volume of material needed to provide strength and stability. As well as saving resources, the flat, lightweight components are easy to transport.

Two planes of a lightweight prefabricated panel are secured together with stainless-steel pins to form a 90-degree component. The pins keep the pieces together during transit and enable horizontal and vertical panels to be fixed in different combinations, creating a personalized furniture unit.

Multiple 90-degree units can be used together, forming a kit of parts to create a flexible interior room. The units and hinged panels can be arranged in many ways to form surfaces for storage, living, working, or sleeping. The resulting interior can be positioned to be freestanding within an open-plan space or to create an enclosed room.

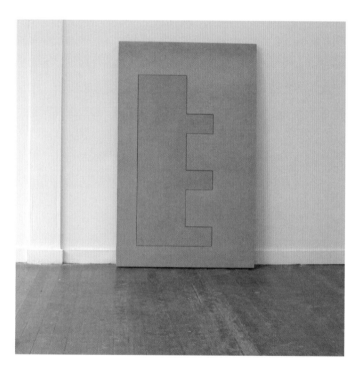

1 Kapteinbolt's 90° Furniture is delivered as two flat-packed panels joined by stainless-steel pins.

2 The panels are opened up to a 90-degree angle to give them stability.

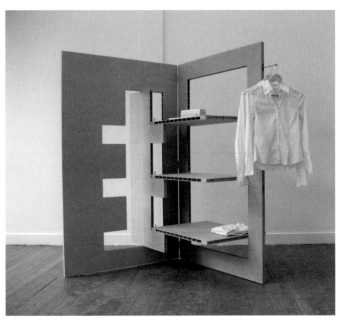

3 Precut planes are folded out from each panel to form shelves and rails.

4 The number and position of shelves can be customized to suit the occupant's needs.

5 Here, four of the double panels are shown joined together to create a whole room. The horizontal surfaces could be used for storage, desks, or a bed, depending on the user's requirements.

CHAPTER 4
PUTTING SUSTAINABILITY INTO PRACTICE

124 INTRODUCING THE PROJECTS

124 TEMPORARY PROJECTS

138 FLEXIBLE PROJECTS

154 LONG-TERM PROJECTS

Introducing the projects

In this chapter, we use exemplar projects to show how the ideas discussed so far in the book can be brought together successfully. The projects demonstrate how a sustainable approach to energy, water, materials, and construction can become an integral part of a good design approach, without compromising on other design concerns, including aesthetics.

The projects are drawn from around the world and feature a variety of designers—be they interior designers, furniture designers, architects, or artists—to source the best examples across a range of contexts. The projects are categorized into the three project types we introduced in Chapter 2: temporary, flexible, and long-term. Thus they cover the broad range of work an interior designer might do, and reflect the different approaches a sustainable interior designer should take to suit the intended longevity or flexibility of the interior.

The projects are analyzed and compared with reference to the key questions relating to a project's life cycle that we discussed in Chapter 2. The analysis reveals the designers' responses to the primary considerations of energy, water, materials, and construction methods. We will see that the approach to these four key issues often varies for temporary, flexible, and long-term projects.

Temporary projects

In this section we discuss the following temporary projects with reference to the key questions we introduced in Chapter 2:

- **ARTEK**, exhibition at Milan Furniture Fair (Italy)

- **BOX PROJECT**, exhibition at 100% Design by Karen Smart and NoChintz, London (UK)

- **KIOSK**, store for SCP by Michael Marriott, London Design Festival (UK)

- **BOMBED MACHÉ**, store for Ksubi by Herbert & Mason, Melbourne (Australia)

- **CHENGDU HUALIN ELEMENTARY SCHOOL** by Shigeru Ban Architects, Chengdu (China)

- **FLASH**, restaurant for the Royal Academy of Arts by David Kohn, London (UK)

Standalone case studies:
- **NOTHING**, office by Alrik Koudenburg & Joost van Bleiswijk, Amsterdam (Netherlands)

- **YESHOP**, store by dARCH Studio, Athens (Greece)

What is the purpose of the project?

Temporary projects could apply to any building type, but are commonplace in the cultural, leisure, and retail sectors. Typical examples are "pop-up" interiors, which appear for a short time, such as exhibitions and installations. The reasons for creating a temporary project can be as diverse as creating a marketing gimmick or providing disaster relief.

The projects showcased in this section range from a school erected in the aftermath of an earthquake, to design exhibitions, an office, pop-up stores, and a pop-up restaurant for the Christmas period. The functions of these projects vary greatly. The purpose of the exhibitions and stores is to showcase a product or brand. For instance, the Artek exhibit showcased the company's sustainability values and its Aalto Stool 60 chair; and Kiosk displayed stock from the store of the same name in New York, which sells everyday products from around the world. The Bombed Maché seeks to make a statement about the usual impermanence of retail design. Flash needed to function effectively as a restaurant, albeit in a temporary capacity. Similarly, Chengdu Hualin Elementary School had to operate successfully as a elementary school, but in trying and unusual circumstances.

Opposite

The Box Project, shown here at 100% Design in London by Karen Smart and NoChintz, is designed to travel from exhibition to exhibition. The box's walls of FSC-certified OSB fold down to form furniture and shelves, enabling the whole interior to be flat-packed for transportation.

Right

Artek's exhibition at the Milan Furniture Fair demonstrates the company's sustainable values, and its furniture and lighting products. The walls are lined with one of Artek's iconic stools.

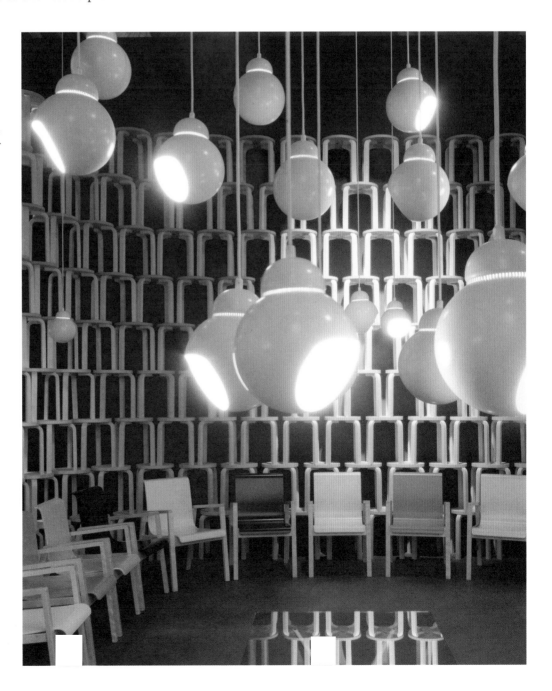

Above
Kiosk, Michael Marriott's pop-up store for SCP, was installed for the London Design Festival. Plastic packaging crates form display tables and a lighting column containing low-energy fluorescent tubes.

Left
Chengdu Hualin Elementary School by Shigeru Ban Architects provided temporary classrooms in the aftermath of an earthquake. The cardboard-tube structure makes the most of locally available materials and can be recycled after use.

Most of the projects are fit-outs or renovations that deal with given spaces. Some, like Flash and Artek, respond intimately to their contexts. Flash creates a room-within-a-room to instill order in the sprawling existing space and enhance its symmetry. An inner envelope is set out to suit the existing windows and cast-iron columns, and subdivided according to Classical proportions, responding to the grandeur of the historic architecture. The inner walls include paintings depicting a fantastical version of nature, beyond a felt trellis, underlining both the site's history as a garden and its present use as an art gallery. Other projects, such as the Bombed Maché and the Box Project, were deliberately self-contained and independent of their settings, so that they could be relocated elsewhere.

Below
Herbert & Mason's Bombed Maché store for Ksubi in Melbourne highlights the transient nature of retail design. Its makeshift cardboard construction can be recycled when no longer needed.

Right
David Kohn's Flash restaurant in London colonized a room at the Royal Academy of Arts over the Christmas period. The wooden packaging crates adorning the walls were stacked for ease of delivery and returned to the supplier for reuse once the restaurant was dismantled.

How long will the interior be required?

By definition, a temporary project will be installed for a brief, finite period. The project's expiry date is usually known at the design stage and must therefore be planned for accordingly.

Artek and the Box Project were installed only for the duration of their host exhibitions: a matter of days or weeks. Kiosk lasted for the duration of the nine-day London Design Festival. Flash was similarly short-lived, providing a novelty destination for three months over the busy festive season. With Chengdu Hualin Elementary School, the time frame was less well defined, as the project would remain in place until a permanent school could be rebuilt.

What energy and water systems are appropriate?

As our projects mostly occupy existing interiors, and generally seek to make little physical impression on their host spaces, altering the energy and water systems is rarely within their scope. In any case, a project that is in place for a very short period will have limited impact on energy and water use during operation compared with other interiors. Nevertheless, where the installations incorporate new lighting they tend to use efficient light fixtures. For instance, the pendant lamps that light the Artek pavilion take low-energy compact-fluorescent lightbulbs; and Kiosk features low-energy fluorescent tubes within its plastic crates.

Pendant lights with low-energy
lightbulbs at the Artek exhibition.

What materials are appropriate?

Cardboard is an extremely popular material for temporary projects, being cheap, strong, lightweight, and easy to obtain. Cardboard also has the advantages of being recycled and recyclable, and reused if it is sourced from packaging, offering the potential to mitigate the environmental impact of short-term interiors. The fact that cardboard is not as durable as more traditional building materials is not a major concern with temporary projects; and coatings can be applied to provide fire and moisture resistance. Our projects show just how versatile cardboard is, fostering creative expression.

Chengdu School is made of cardboard tubes, which were readily available on site and provided a cheap, quick solution appropriate to an emergency situation. The Bombed Maché also creates an entire structure out of cardboard, but as an installation within an existing interior. Here, cardboard is appropriate because it is an unexpected material in the showy world of fashion and retail that highlights our throwaway culture. In contrast to most retail interiors, the Bombed Maché is formed of 80% reclaimed materials.

Other packaging materials are also ideal materials for temporary projects, providing cheap reclaimed materials that can be reused. The inner walls in Flash are made of wooden crates, usually used for packaging artwork, sourced from a local, London-based, company. Kiosk includes display tables and columns of shelving formed of stacked plastic crates.

Simple wood products supplement packaging materials in many of the designs. The tabletops and display boards at Kiosk are made of plywood. The Box Project is made entirely from FSC-certified oriented strand board (OSB), formed of locally sourced forestry waste and produced locally. The chairs at Artek are made of birch plywood.

Left
The Bombed Maché uses cardboard as an unconventional material for a retail environment.

Above
Flash's walls are lined with wooden packaging crates.

What construction methods are appropriate?

The projects tend to use lightweight, freestanding construction methods that will leave little trace on the site once they are gone. Many, like the Box Project and the Bombed Maché, barely touch the existing building shell, but form standalone objects within the space.

Many of the designs had to consider ease of transportation, both to reach the site for installation, and to move on to another site for reuse. Kiosk's lightweight plastic crates can be simply stacked together for delivery, while the flat plywood sheets are easily transported. The packaging crates used in Flash are also stackable for ease of delivery. The Box Project is conceived as a box that furnishes itself: panels in the box's walls fold down to create seating, tables, and shelves. This means the whole interior can be flat-packed into five pieces that fit into a van, as well as ensuring the design uses materials economically. Artek's exhibition shows a similar economy of materials, as the chairs that are being displayed double as the wall covering: 750 stools line the walls. The stools can be stacked together for transportation.

Lightweight and flat-pack solutions are also quick and simple to put together on site, which is crucial as temporary projects are often built to tight construction

The Bombed Maché consists of a freestanding cardboard structure within an existing corridor.

schedules. The exhibitions have all been designed to be installed quickly, often between a previous exhibition finishing and the new exhibition opening. For instance, erecting the Box Project only requires manpower. Similarly, the crates at Kiosk can be stacked together by hand and combined with horizontal or vertical planes of plywood to create a variety of display units. The Bombed Maché's handcrafted construction gives the structure a deliberate cut-and-pasted character, drawing attention to the perception of cardboard as a scrap material. Flash's crates are stacked together in different orientations, creating a varied effect of flat horizontal or vertical faces and deep recesses. Simple building methods were also essential for Chengdu School, as the project was to be assembled by unskilled volunteers.

The construction methods have been chosen with a view to being easy to disassemble. At Kiosk, metal hooks hold the components in place and can be easily detached, while the Box Project can simply be folded back up.

Top
Chengdu School's simple construction techniques meant that it could be built by volunteers.

Above
The walls of Artek's exhibition are lined with 750 stools, so the products on display create the wall covering.

How will the space function?

A common thread linking these temporary projects is that they are designed to provoke thought among their users about materials, construction methods, and waste. Their prominent expression of unconventional building materials encourages visitors to question our customary approach to packaging and cheap materials, showing they can be reused practically, wittily, and beautifully. Clearly, Chengdu School puts this thinking to a very practical application, borne of necessity, showing that cheap, commonplace materials and simple construction methods can provide effective solutions to major human problems.

Flexibility in use is central to the Box Project, which can accommodate a variety of uses. As well as working as an exhibition stand, it can be used as a pop-up bar, retail unit, or gallery. The Bombed Maché is equally versatile, simultaneously functioning as an art installation, store, and gallery.

Packaging materials offered a cheap, readily available building material for Chengdu School.

What will happen to it when it is no longer useful?

Clearly, temporary projects need a definite solution to their ultimate fate, as it is known that they will not be needed in the near future.

Many of the designers planned for components to be reused. The stools that line the walls of the Artek pavilion could be taken down and sold as usual after the exhibition. The crates from Kiosk were sold to be used as storage boxes, shelving, or bicycle baskets. The cladding panels, crockery, and chandelier in Flash were also intended for sale once the restaurant ceased to be.

With the Box Project, the whole exhibit is designed for reuse, and transported to other sites to be used over and over again.

Flash's furniture was used again for events, and the crates that formed the walls were returned to the supplier to be reused as packaging. Similarly, the plywood tabletops in the SCP Kiosk were reused elsewhere.

Those projects made of cardboard, including Chengdu School and the Bombed Maché, can be taken apart for recycling, or reused if the cardboard is still in good condition.

After use, the packaging crates used in Kiosk were sold as storage boxes, shelving, and bicycle baskets.

Case study Temporary project 1

Nothing advertising agency, Amsterdam (Netherlands) by Alrik Koudenburg and Joost van Bleiswijk

Alrik Koudenburg and Joost van Bleiswijk designed this office fit-out in Amsterdam to last for two years, after which the lease on the existing building expired. The design suits these short-term circumstances and the quirky style of its occupants—advertising agency Nothing.

The project is treated as a structure within a structure, forming an isolated "fortress." It is self-supporting, rather than being fixed to the fabric of the existing building, so it can be removed at the end of its life without leaving any trace. The only structure is the wooden poles that support the stairs and platform for the partners' office.

The temporary structure is constructed of cardboard, with precisely cut slotted joints to avoid the need for screws and glue. As a result, the 1,500 individual pieces can be quickly dismantled and packed flat for recycling or transportation for reuse when the lease expires. Industrial

⅝in (15mm)-thick recycled honeycomb cardboard is used, and is varnished to protect it from damage from spilled drinks.

Electric wiring and fluorescent lighting tubes, chosen for their energy efficiency, are concealed within the cardboard structure.

The office embraces the spirit of fun that is often a feature of temporary projects. The rough and ready cardboard is unashamedly expressed. It is the only material used, other than the MDF flooring that was chosen to look like cardboard but give sufficient durability, and the wooden poles. The cardboard is meant to provoke a reaction from the agency's visitors. Further, staff are encouraged to customize the surfaces by drawing ideas and doodles on them, creating a giant sketchbook. The use of waste cardboard fits the agency's philosophy of creating something out of nothing—indeed, the cardboard joints are

playfully elaborate, elevating this basic material and giving the interior an extravagant feel.

Parts of the interior can be replaced cheaply if they get damaged, and the structure can simply be added to or amended if the company expands. During their first year, the Nothing team grew and were able to alter part of the structure to add more desks into the existing framework.

Above
The cardboard structure can easily be removed at the end of its life. The structure avoids touching the existing building. Even the floor is made to look like cardboard, and staff can draw over the walls.

Above
The lightweight cardboard construction with slotted joints requires no connectors or glue for ease of deconstruction.

Below
The structure is freestanding and entirely made of cardboard, except for hidden wooden poles supporting this platform for the partners' office.

Above
This office makes the most of the opportunity to have fun with a temporary project, which is apt for advertising agency Nothing's creative approach.

Case study Temporary project 2

Yeshop boutique, Athens (Greece) by dARCH Studio

Left
Existing furniture is screwed to the walls to free up the floor space. Tables are reused as light shades and bookcases form display shelving. Corrugated cardboard sheets form a wall covering.

Below
Corrugated cardboard sheets are glued together in layers over the existing walls to give a three-dimensional effect.

Yeshop, a boutique in Athens for fashion designer Yiorgos Eleftheriades, was created for a two-year maximum lifespan, because the store interior is often refreshed. The design by dARCH Studio allows for this and takes inspiration from Eleftheriades's preference for working with natural and environmentally friendly fabrics.

The simple design, using cheap and found materials, has dramatically transformed the interior. The existing furniture has been fixed to the walls to create an inventive new look: bookcases are turned into display shelving, while tables are used as light shades to conceal recessed lighting. The walls have been covered in corrugated cardboard sourced from packaging. This forms a corduroy-textured wallpaper behind the repurposed furniture.

Against another wall, corrugated cardboard sheets have been pasted together in layers, creating a three-dimensional curved form. The cardboard sheets were cut and laid by hand, giving a handcrafted feel. The resulting sculptural shape is intended to represent the curves of the body being dressed in clothes made from two-dimensional patterns, symbolizing the fashion designer's work. Display boxes made from OSB are set into the curve.

As well as reusing packaging and furniture, Yeshop reuses flooring and gypsum wall board from the previous interior. These elements were retained, but covered or painted where necessary to refresh their appearance.

Flexibility in use is important, as the space is often used as an exhibition area, lounge, party venue, and for fashion shows when not operating as a store. Focusing the design interventions on the walls kept the floor space clear of obstructions to enable these diverse uses, while still creating a cozy atmosphere.

The interior decoration can easily be removed to make way for the next design. The layers of cardboard are glued to the existing walls, so the construction can be stripped away to reveal the original background when the store owner wants to redecorate the interior. Long-lasting, efficient fluorescent lighting has been chosen, so that it can be retained in the next renovation. The furniture can be taken down and reused as originally intended, while the cardboard can be stripped away and recycled.

Top
Back-lit display shelving for accessories is recessed into the cardboard wall covering.

Above
The design is inspired by the resident fashion designer's use of sustainable fabrics.

Flexible projects

In this section we use the key questions introduced in Chapter 2 to compare the following flexible projects:

- **INCUBATION**, store by Matt Gibson Architecture + Design, Melbourne (Australia)

- **NIKE EAST LONDON 1948**, store by Wilson Brothers, London (UK)

- **SMITHFIELD**, store by Burnt Toast, Manchester (UK)

- **NORTH**, office by Skylab Architecture, Portland (US)

- **COUNTRY SCHOOL PREFAB**, school by Office of Mobile Design, Valley Village (US)

Standalone case studies:
- **ELGAR ROOM**, restaurant-cum-events space for Royal Albert Hall by Jestico + Whiles, London (UK)

- **HOWIES**, store by Remodel, Bristol (UK)

Opposite

Matt Gibson Architecture + Design's Incubation store in Melbourne revives a disused corridor of a shopping mall. It has built-in flexibility to suit short lets, enabled by sturdy OSB components.

Below

The Smithfield store by Burnt Toast in Manchester used cardboard mailing tubes and shipping boxes to create a striking interior. The boxes can be readily arranged to transform the space.

Country School Prefab in Valley Village by Office of Mobile Design consists of prefabricated pavilions erected in a school playground. The buildings can be moved or removed easily to suit the school's changing needs.

What is the purpose of the project?

Flexible projects can fall within any building sector, but are common in retail, where frequent change is desirable to keep up with changing fashions. Any project can have flexible aspects, but our demonstration projects have flexibility at their core, informing the designers' thinking throughout. They are dominated by clothes stores, but also include a school and an office.

With the exception of Country School Prefab, all of these projects are renovations or fit-outs, involving the challenges of working within existing buildings or shells.

The different functions of the projects influence the design requirements and therefore the sustainable measures that are feasible. The retail units, office, and school are used primarily during the day, whereas Nike 1948 contains broader functions that mean it is used both by day and night. The school is clearly intended for children; the fashion stores are geared toward young people; and the office caters for creative professionals.

Some of the projects must suit more than one function. Nike 1948 acts as a retail space, showroom, music venue, and base for running clubs. Within Country School Prefab there are also multifunctional spaces, such as an art space that doubles as a community room.

The designs create an appropriate character for each project. In retail, it is important that the look of the interior expresses the brand. Thus, the store for sportswear retailer Nike needed a sporty, youthful feel. A vibrant, creative atmosphere was an important requirement for North, which is home to a branding agency. In Country School Prefab, the aesthetic style was not so predetermined, so long as the designer created a stimulating, didactic environment for the pupils.

Below
Skylab's North office in Portland occupies a former printworks, filling it with modular structures that promote flexible working.

Right
Nike East London 1948 by Wilson Brothers is used day and night—as a store, showroom, music venue, and running club—requiring very little redesign.

How long will the interior be required?

The merit of flexible projects is that they should extend the life of the interior by being able to adapt to change, be this to keep pace with fashion, company branding, technology, growth of the organization, new tenants, or a change in function of the interior. Despite this, it is important to establish how long the interior is likely to remain in its present form and to consider what will happen to its components when unforeseeable change eventually renders it unsuitable.

How long the interior remains as installed will depend on whether its flexibility is intended to address short- or long-term changes. The store interiors are typically expected to last a couple of years, until fashions and wear demand they be refreshed. The Incubation store is aimed at short leases, allowing new owners to reconfigure the basic structure to suit their needs. Incubation, and the Nike 1948 and Smithfield stores, also allow for more frequent changes, as their underlying structure can be rearranged to create different displays. The Country School Prefab is intended for longer-term change: its modular construction can be extended or relocated to accommodate future needs.

What energy and water systems are appropriate?

Using daylight was particularly important in Country School Prefab to create pleasant, well-lit study spaces, using large windows, high ceilings, and light-colored surfaces. Here, the windows are also designed to allow natural cross-ventilation, ensuring fresh air and comfortable working conditions for the children. Similarly, North makes good use of the existing large windows of a former printworks to ensure good daylighting and comfortable working conditions within the office. Desks and meeting rooms are positioned near windows, and a high-level, cantilevered meeting room takes advantage of the clerestory windows. In both projects, energy-efficient systems back up these passive design measures. Country School Prefab includes low-energy lighting, while North has a highly efficient boiler and air-conditioning system.

Nike's efficient lighting comes in the form of fluorescent tubes that create the outline of a sports pitch and compass above the space, while the light fixtures at Smithfield were reclaimed.

Most of the projects are installations within larger developments and do not therefore need dedicated water systems. However, North has been fitted with dual-flush toilets to save water and Country School Prefab sets out to teach the schoolchildren about saving water.

High, sloping ceilings and white surfaces at Country School Prefab allow light, both from the windows and low-energy light fixtures, to fill the classrooms.

Left
Country School Prefab's large windows admit plenty of natural daylight and encourage cross-ventilation.

Above
North office includes a cantilevered meeting room that is raised above the main office to receive daylight from the existing clerestory windows.

What materials are appropriate?

Office of Mobile Design was keen to use natural, low-emitting materials at Country School Prefab to contribute to a healthy interior for pupils and their teachers. Bamboo and blended cork and recycled-rubber flooring were used. Along with formaldehyde-free fiberboard wall cladding, they provide natural and practical surfaces. The furniture includes cabinets formed of biofiber-composite panels made from sunflower seed husks.

The materials used in the Smithfield menswear store in Manchester had to be affordable but able to create a quirky effect. Designer Burnt Toast also wanted the materials to be both 100% recycled and from local sources. Cardboard mailing tubes and shipping boxes from a local mill have been ingeniously reused to form wall coverings, light fixtures, clothing displays, and animal sculptures. Furthermore, the wooden structure supporting the cardboard came from a reclaimed wood supplier in Manchester.

Recycled products also feature at Nike 1948, where a fully recycled rubber sports surface forms the floor covering. The recycled rubber is partly sourced from the soles of old sneakers, helping tackle disposal of the store's products at the end of their life.

All of the projects offering short-term flexibility rely on robust, lightweight materials that are easy to move but will not get damaged in the process. This is especially true of the shelving at Nike 1948 and the cardboard display boxes at Smithfield. Meanwhile, Incubation uses OSB to create a sturdy shell that can withstand the frequent adjustments that take place within it.

Below
These cabinets at Country School Prefab are made from sunflower seed husks.

Below right
The Smithfield store is made from cardboard packaging, such as these shipping boxes arranged to display shoes. Witty animal sculptures, like the panda head on the wall, have also been fashioned from cardboard.

The existing railroad arches create a dramatic space in Nike 1948.

What construction methods are appropriate?

The renovation projects make use of the existing structure. At Nike 1948, the historic railroad arches overhead have been exploited to create a dramatic, curved ceiling, and the existing brick walls provide an appealing backdrop to the modern interior. Likewise, the shell of the printworks gives a distinctive character to North's interior.

The construction methods, in combination with the materials used, support the flexible nature of the interiors. Nike 1948 has a modular system of steel and plywood display units that can be reconfigured in different layouts to transform the space. These are inspired by grandstand seating and have wheels so they can be easily rearranged: the numerous potential combinations comprise display tables for the store mode and auditorium seating for events. Detachable hanging clothing rods offer additional flexibility at high level.

A similar outcome is achieved in the Smithfield interior using self-supporting cardboard structures that can be stacked and arranged in multiple ways. Incubation has randomly placed hinged or stayed flaps that can be fully or partly opened for display, as well as alternative entrance positions, and an optional folding wall to subdivide the space for up to three tenants.

Incubation was built in a shopping mall's disused corridor; its self-supporting steel frame, stiffened with OSB, was chosen to avoid the need to attach to the existing shell. This simple, efficient construction is honestly expressed.

North's freestanding modular structures avoid the need to touch or attach to the historic building, other than at floor level, meaning the office interior can simply be moved or removed without leaving a trace. This suits the project's conception as an expedition base camp composed of portable elements.

Steel-framed modules create a portable solution at Country School Prefab. The standardized construction allowed the module to be repeated efficiently, creating three similar spaces to absorb the school's expansion.

Opposite
Nike 1948's display units can be moved around on their wheels to allow different uses of the space.

Above and right
Incubation's hinged flaps can be opened or closed to create different display layouts. The interior can be subdivided, creating up to three stores.

How will the space function?

With flexibility in use being key, all these projects had to carefully consider how this would be enabled. We have already seen how the choices of energy systems, materials, and construction methods have been guided by this thinking. At Nike 1948 and Smithfield, this allows the store owners to refresh the interiors at their whim. At Incubation, it means the interior can be adapted to suit different types of retail outlets and numbers of retail tenants. And at Country School Prefab and Nike 1948, it allows spaces to be used for multiple activities.

North is intended to foster an unconventional way of working attuned to the creative approach of the branding agency it accommodates. Its modular structures, based around social activities such as cooking, eating, lounging, and gaming, encourage staff to collaborate and interact away from static workstations, adopting flexible working patterns.

Above
Incubation's linear design means that it can be subdivided to accommodate several retail tenants, while its adjustable walls can be adapted to suit different types of store.

Below
North office's design supports unorthodox working patterns by providing social areas in which staff can work together.

What will happen to it when it is no longer useful?

The built-in flexibility of these projects should ensure a long life, but the designers have still considered how to avoid them ending up as landfill when they are no longer needed.

Many of the fit-out and renovation projects can simply be removed and reassembled elsewhere without any lasting impact on their host spaces. The space that Nike 1948 has colonized is on a short lease, but the small, lightweight components mean the design can easily be taken away. The same is true for Incubation, as this freestanding object can be easily removed without causing any damage to its surroundings. North's modules can be removed without affecting the historic building, and its pine paneling and steel panels can be reused.

Country School Prefab is also portable and the cabins can be removed from the playground they were installed on.

The projects tend to use recyclable materials and simple construction methods to allow them to be dismantled for recycling if they cannot be reused. For example, the cardboard used throughout the Smithfield store can be readily recycled, as can the modules used at North.

Above
Country School Prefab consists of cabins installed within the existing school playground, which can be taken away when no longer required.

Left
The new elements in North office do not touch the existing building's ceilings or walls, allowing them to be removed easily later.

Case study Flexible project 1

The Elgar Room, Royal Albert Hall, London (UK) by Jestico + Whiles

The Elgar Room at the Royal Albert Hall in London is a classic example of a flexible interior, functioning as either a restaurant with more than 100 covers or a multipurpose events space for 350 people. Designer Jestico + Whiles created an interior with built-in flexibility, despite the constraints of working within a historic building.

The simple design solution allows the historic space to form a static backdrop, using a monochrome color palette to highlight its elegant proportions. An existing, nonoriginal stage has been removed to reveal the full height of the windows and restore the room to its original proportions. The building's thermal performance has been improved by adding solar-control double glazing to the windows and lining the roof space with insulation. Efficiency improvements have been achieved by installing low-energy lighting and building systems, and energy- and water-saving appliances.

Meanwhile, simple day-to-day changes to the lighting, furniture, and fixtures transform the atmosphere of the space to suit its use. This is easily achieved using color-changing LED lighting, movable sound and lighting equipment, interchangeable drapes, and lightweight, stackable tables and chairs in a selection of different colors.

Materials have been chosen for minimal environmental impact, including recycled gypsum acoustic flooring, water-based paints, and FSC-certified wood and plywood.

Opposite
Here the space is used as a restaurant, with subtle, white lighting and the blinds raised to admit daylight. The lightweight chairs and tables can be easily moved and stacked together. The three different chair fabrics allow the chairs to be rearranged to create a different look and their warm, bright colors give the restaurant a welcoming feel.

Right
When used for intimate rock gigs, the chairs and tables are removed and stored elsewhere in the building. Bright-colored background lighting is used—and the colors changed throughout the performance to create the right mood—and the blinds are lowered to create blackout. Show lighting and speakers mounted on ceiling tracks are positioned to create the desired effect.

Below right
The room accommodates a variety of other events, including comedy, cabaret, theater, and conferences. Here, bright pink lighting fills the space and creates the right atmosphere for an after-show party.

Case study Flexible project 2

Howies store, Bristol (UK) by Remodel

The Howies store in Bristol, designed by Remodel, allows for both short- and long-term flexibility. The Bristol store is the second in casual clothing company Howies' expansion from online and mail-order retailing to actual stores. The interior highlights the retailer's sustainable approach to business and allows for its anticipated growth.

A large existing building was chosen for the project to allow the retail area to grow organically in tandem with the business. From the outset, the whole building was fitted out and essential systems, such as electric wiring, were installed throughout, ensuring that expansion would be simple and immediate.

Daily flexibility is provided through multiuse spaces, and changeable furniture and fixtures. The Denim Room, where jeans are displayed on trestle tables and hung from the ceiling rafters, is partly enclosed by glazed walls. This transparency retains a visual connection with the rest of the store, but the glazed doors can be closed to enable the room to be used for lectures or as an art gallery.

In the main store area, all of the display furniture is either portable or adjustable. Freestanding crates, A-frames, benches, and trestle tables are used to display clothes in the center of the space and can easily be moved or removed to create different layouts. Around the room's perimeter, clothing rods and exhibition displays are fixed into continuous horizontal and vertical tracks, so they can be slid into alternative locations. Elsewhere, clothes are suspended from metal hangers over the rafters above and can be relocated. The light fixtures can readily be adjusted to suit changes in the layout, as the background lighting is on a track system and each light fixture can be tilted to change its direction. Remodel replaced an inefficient lighting system with a low level of ambient lighting, supplemented by energy-efficient halide spotlights for accent lighting.

Existing materials found on site were reused, including a wall clad in glazed tiles that was uncovered beneath layers of gypsum wall board. Reclaimed wood from nearby suppliers was used to create the display units, and gives the interior a cozy character that suits the Howies brand.

Above
The Denim Room can be closed off from the main store floor by glass doors, allowing it to double as a lecture room or gallery space.

Opposite
Clothing is hung from the ceiling rafters in the Denim Room, using metal hangers that can be moved or removed to suit requirements. Adjustable spotlights are mounted on a track system along the rafters.

Left
The main store area can be reconfigured to allow different layouts. Freestanding display units, including A-frames and crates, are used toward the center of the space. Around the perimeter, horizontal clothes rods connect to a track system. Light fixtures are on a ceiling-mounted track system and their angle can be adjusted.

Above
Displays in the store highlight the company's sustainable philosophy.

Long-term projects

We will now analyze the following long-term projects using the key questions we introduced in Chapter 2:

- **MOSS HOUSE**, house by Nendo, Tokyo (Japan)

- **BALEHAUS**, house by White Design, Bath (UK)

- **KOBY COTTAGE**, house by Garrison Architects, Albion (US)

- **ELWOOD CLOTHING**, office by Matt Gibson Architecture + Design, Melbourne (Australia)

- **GARDEN MUSEUM**, by Dow Jones Architects, London (UK)

- **GREENHOUSE**, nightclub by Bluarch, New York (US)

- **CLUB WATT**, nightclub by Studio Roosegaarde, Rotterdam (Netherlands)

- **NATURE CAFÉ LA PORTE**, restaurant by RAU architects, Amsterdam (Netherlands)

Standalone case studies:
- **DESIGN COUNCIL**, offices by Clive Sall Architecture and Carl Turner Architects, London (UK)

- **RENCTAS**, store by Domo Arquitetos Associados, Brasilia (Brazil)

BaleHaus in Bath, a prototype house by White Design. This new-build project enabled a comprehensive approach to sustainable design, including high levels of insulation within the external walls.

What is the purpose of the project?

Typically, long-term interior projects will be for the residential, leisure, education, healthcare, and commercial sectors. Our exemplar projects include houses, nightclubs, an office, a museum, a store, and a café.

Many of these projects, including Moss House and the Garden Museum, renovated existing spaces and had to find innovative ways to work within a given environment. At the Garden Museum this involved inserting a freestanding belvedere structure to make full use of the double-height interior of an existing church. A different approach was taken at Moss House, where the interior was transformed largely through decoration. Other projects, such as Koby Cottage and BaleHaus, are fit-outs or entirely new buildings, allowing a freer reign and a more holistic approach.

Top
Nendo's Moss House in Tokyo takes inspiration from nature to reinvigorate an existing residential interior.

Above
The refurbished Garden Museum in London by Dow Jones Architects transforms an existing church interior using prefabricated wooden panels. The new lighting uses low-energy lightbulbs.

The interiors have been designed for quite different activities, the practical requirements for a nightclub being markedly different from those for a private house. The functions dictate when the spaces will be used: nightclubs will be used mainly after dark, when offices are likely to be empty. And they have been designed for quite different users: Koby Cottage is a tranquil retreat for relatives to spend time with young people who are in care, while Nature Café La Porte serves passersby in a railroad station. The private houses were generally designed for owners who want a sustainable lifestyle, whereas some of the staff working in the office might be less committed to protecting the environment. Moreover, the housing projects are intended for small families, whereas public buildings such as nightclubs and cafés must cater for large groups of people. Club Watt is intended to teach young people about sustainable living, in a refreshingly light-hearted way.

The ambience achieved by each design suits its purpose. Both nightclubs have aspired to a futuristic, sophisticated look, created with LED lighting. The Elwood Clothing office has a far rougher, more traditional appearance to express the jeans company's "Tomorrow's Vintage" motto through an interior that is obviously made of reused elements.

Above left
Nature Café La Porte in Amsterdam by RAU architects serves organic food and drink in an Amsterdam railroad station.

Left
Koby Cottage by Garrison Architects in Albion capitalizes on its bucolic setting to provide a peaceful retreat for families visiting young people in care. Views and daylight dominate the interior of this prefabricated building.

Opposite
Matt Gibson Architecture + Design's Melbourne office for Elwood Clothing is a conversion of a former warehouse. Its rough, traditional look reflects Elwood Clothing's vintage jeans brand.

How long will the interior be required?

Long-term projects are those that, once completed, are expected to remain more or less as designed for many years. Of course, the interiors are likely to be redecorated and repaired over this long time span, but the underlying design solution and its function will remain intact.

For long-term projects, it is merely necessary to recognize that they need to last for an extensive period of time, but will eventually become obsolete. We will see that these facts, combined with the interior's purpose, inform the approach to the remaining questions.

What energy and water systems are appropriate?

The long-term projects rightly take energy and water use seriously, acknowledging that the benefits of low-energy and water-saving design will be apparent for many years.

The energy systems must be tuned to the interior's purpose, and there is no better demonstration than Club Watt. Here, the movement of people on the dance floor generates electricity for use within the space. Both Club Watt and the Greenhouse nightclub make much use of LEDs for lighting. LEDs allow dramatic color changes but produce relatively low illumination, which is perfect for a darkened nightclub. As they are long-lasting, energy-efficient, and seldom require maintenance, LEDs are an apt choice for long-term projects. Crystals hung from the ceiling in Greenhouse reflect light around the space to boost illumination levels.

Above left
Studio Roosegaarde's Club Watt nightclub in Rotterdam aims to educate young people about sustainability.

Above right
Colored LED lights are housed in the dance floor at Club Watt.

Left
Club Watt's LEDs change color in response to people's movement on the dance floor.

Opposite
Greenhouse's LED lights change color and reflect off crystals suspended from the nightclub's ceiling.

Daylight is much more important in interiors, such as offices, that are used throughout the day. The existing sawtooth roof was reopened to allow more daylight into the Elwood Clothing offices, and low partitions and glazed walls allow the light to travel deep into the space. Moss House's mirrors ensure that light is reflected around the interior, while BaleHaus includes a sun pipe to bring light through the roof space and into the stairs.

Left
A sun pipe brings daylight and sunlight into the stairwell of BaleHaus.

Below
Partly glazed walls and white surfaces at Elwood Clothing maximize light within the cellular spaces.

Mirrors and white-painted surfaces are used within Moss House to make the most of daylight from the large existing windows.

The new-build projects are most able to exploit passive design. Koby Cottage and BaleHaus use plenty of insulation, made of straw in the latter, to boost the thermal performance of the building envelope. But even renovations can employ passive design: RAU formed glass openings within existing solid walls at Nature Café La Porte to let in daylight and sunlight to light and heat the space.

Energy efficiency is demonstrated at Koby Cottage by its heating and cooling system, which uses heat exchange, and its efficient and nonpolluting ethanol-burning fireplace. All new lighting at the Garden Museum is low-energy. Here, a simple system of reusing indoor air, which is of fairly constant temperature and humidity thanks to the church's high thermal mass, provides ventilation with minimal energy input. At Club Watt, drinks are stored in basement tanks to minimize the energy needed to keep them cool.

Several of the projects include renewable energy, showing that it is often viable for long-term projects. The method is especially innovative at Nature Café La

New glazing was added to Nature Café La Porte to improve daylight penetration.

Porte where, as customers enter by pushing the revolving entrance door, they generate enough energy for their cup of coffee. On top of this, solar panels heat the café's hot water, while a wind turbine and photovoltaic panels will be added in the future. The design for Koby Cottage has a bolt-on option for photovoltaic roof panels, recognizing that renewable technologies may not be affordable to everyone.

Several of the long-term projects aim to limit water use over their lifetime. This was paramount in the nightclubs, where a high turnover of drinking visitors means the toilets are used often. Toilets are flushed with harvested rainwater in Club Watt, and Greenhouse has waterless urinals and dual-flush toilets.

Nature Café La Porte's revolving door generates electricity every time customers pass through it.

What materials are appropriate?

Again, the interior's purpose should inform the palette of materials used. As Koby Cottage sets out to create a therapeutic environment for families, it was important to the designer to pick natural materials, such as the maple that covers the floors, walls, and ceilings. Similarly, Nature Café La Porte features natural materials, including wood, that promote clean air and reflect its health-conscious mission of selling organic food and drink. Salvaged wooden floorboards at Elwood Clothing underline the brand's focus on vintage.

All long-term projects need to use robust materials that will withstand years of wear. In public buildings that experience a lot of pedestrian traffic, this is especially pertinent. The Garden Museum's engineered wood is lightweight yet strong, and also avoids the need for a surface finish. Elwood Clothing's self-finished brick walls are extremely robust and maintenance-free.

Natural materials like wood dominate Nature Café La Porte's interior.

Below
Elwood Clothing has a reclaimed wood floor behind the reception.

Bottom
Exposed existing brick walls at Elwood Clothing avoid the need for a surface finish.

The projects occasionally capitalize on their longevity to justify using materials with high embodied energy where they will bring other environmental benefits over the lifetime of the project. For example, Koby Cottage uses high-performance synthetic insulation and a steel structure. Still, the projects seek to limit embodied energy overall by using local materials. BaleHaus uses a wooden frame filled with straw (a by-product of wheat production), covered with lime plaster, all sourced locally.

Some of the projects use reclaimed or recycled materials. Elwood Clothing's wooden floor is reclaimed. Koby Cottage includes recycled-porcelain floor tiles and its steel-framed structure has a high recycled content. Greenhouse includes recycled-content vinyl.

Clearly wood is a popular choice among the projects, so it is reassuring that this has been responsibly sourced where it could not be reclaimed. The maple used on Koby Cottage's floors, walls, and ceilings is FSC-certified. The engineered wood balustrade in the Garden Museum comes from well-managed European plantations that regenerate quickly. Greenhouse nightclub uses the renewable species boxwood and, as an alternative to wood, fast-growing bamboo covers the walls and floors.

Opposite
Koby Cottage's materials include renewable wooden floor, ceiling, and wall coverings.

Above
Greenhouse uses bamboo as a floor and wall covering.

What construction methods are appropriate?

The renovation projects have made use of the existing structure where possible. The Garden Museum successfully revives an oversized extant structure, keeping all of the original envelope. Elwood Clothing's designers transformed a disused industrial warehouse by removing unwanted layers to reveal characterful steel roof trusses, concrete floors, and brickwork walls.

Many of the projects celebrate modern methods of construction, taking advantage of their benefits in minimizing construction times, controlling construction quality and durability, and reducing waste. The Garden Museum's engineered-wood belvedere consists of prefabricated wooden panels, clearly distinguishing the new construction from the existing building and allowing the two to be reverently detached from each other. The new-build Koby Cottage uses prefabricated modular steel construction for the whole structure. Hollow tubular steel makes the modules lightweight, and all internal fixtures, including the kitchen, were installed before delivery to the site. BaleHaus combines modern construction processes with natural materials in its straw-based prefabricated wall panels.

The original warehouse trusses and sloping ceiling have been revealed at Elwood Clothing.

Above
The Garden Museum's belvedere is made of prefabricated wooden panels and forms a mezzanine gallery that blends in with the historic church setting.

Left
BaleHaus uses traditional natural materials in a modern way, its walls being made of prefabricated straw and wooden panels.

How will the space function?

Flexibility is built into Koby Cottage, which has a banquette seat with removable cushions that can be transformed into a daybed, saving space. The Garden Museum had to accommodate permanent and temporary exhibits, as well as frequent lectures, seminars, and debates. Raising the permanent collection onto a mezzanine means that the ground floor space, used as a temporary gallery, can be quickly cleared for events. Greenhouse also has integral flexibility, serving as an events space when not operating as a nightclub.

The designers have all tried to encourage people to act in ways that consider the environment. The Elwood Clothing offices are planned so that regularly used spaces and workspaces, which need plenty of light, are placed near windows or roof lights to discourage unnecessary use of electric lighting. In the residential projects, areas occupied more during the day, such as BaleHaus and Koby Cottage's living and dining areas, have been positioned near glazing. And Koby Cottage includes generous bicycle storage.

At Club Watt, sustainable living is made a fun part of the whole experience. Clubbers are immersed in environmentally conscious design, from drinks served in recyclable plastic cups, to local organic food, to visible transparent pipes carrying recycled rainwater to flush the toilets—and of course the interactive dance floor allowing dancers to control the LEDs. Visitors experience a much more sedate interpretation of sustainability at Koby Cottage, being surrounded by natural materials and views of nature. A courtyard and green roof at Club Watt allow clubbers to relax amid nature. In a more abstract way, Moss House's wallpaper embossed with vivid green dried moss constantly reminds its occupants of the natural world and perhaps their duty to it. Greenhouse's whole interior is conceived as a landscape, with wooden animal sculptures, a bar representing a miniature landscape, and a wavelike crystal ceiling.

Some of the designers returned to site once the completed interior was in use to check that things were working as planned. For example, formal post-occupancy studies were made at BaleHaus, where performance is being monitored for one year.

Below left
Locating the permanent exhibition at mezzanine level frees up the ground floor of the Garden Museum for events.

Below
Animal sculptures on the tables in Greenhouse nightclub are a reminder of the natural world, while the crystal ceiling suggests a wave.

What will happen to it when it is no longer useful?

Although the projects are long-term ones, their designers have been far-sighted enough to consider their end.

BaleHaus is designed for reuse, as its robust, modular wall panels can each be removed in one piece and transported to another site for reinstallation. Alternatively, the panels' individual components can be reused.

The next best approach, of designing for recycling, was taken at the Garden Museum. Its new belvedere deliberately avoids touching the church, other than at floor level, so that it can be removed without damaging the existing building. Upon removal, the engineered-wood structure could be recycled as fuel to heat 12 homes for one year. Recyclable materials, including glass and wood, are used within Greenhouse and BaleHaus. Koby Cottage includes a daybed upholstered with biodegradable fabric that can be composted at the end of its life.

This chapter has shown that sustainable interior design can be put into practice with impressive results. The showcased projects demonstrate that beautiful designs with low environmental impact are achievable in a range of contexts, no matter what the building type or location. Each designer has simply applied a sustainable design approach befitting the expected duration of their project.

The new structure does not touch the existing construction at the Garden Museum, skimming past the church's columns and walls.

Case study Long-term project 1

Design Council headquarters, London (UK) by Clive Sall Architecture and Carl Turner Architects

Above
On the ground floor, the wooden "hedges" and "train" organize the space, creating a variety of working areas. Functional parts of the existing interior, such as the lighting and office furniture, have been incorporated in the new design.

Right
The first-floor "hedge" includes an open meeting area, shelves, and recesses. Notices are fixed into the wood.

Clive Sall Architecture and Carl Turner Architects remodeled the Design Council's headquarters in London to last as long as possible. This was achieved, on a limited budget, by scrutinizing the functionality of the existing office, allowing for flexibility in how the spaces would be used and specifying durable materials.

The design team carefully studied the existing interior and observed the working patterns of the occupants to identify the office's strengths and shortcomings. The resulting design retained the functional parts of the existing fit-out—including desks, lamps, kitchen tiles, and bulletin boards— seamlessly incorporating them into the new interior. For example, new life is breathed into the existing carpet tiles by relaying them in new combinations to create patterns where they have worn to different degrees. In addition, a cycle store and shower have been added to address current needs. Where new systems were needed, the designers seized the opportunity to improve the interior's energy performance, choosing low-voltage lighting linked to movement sensors.

The interior includes flexible items to help it accommodate changes in how it is used, prolonging its life. The exhibition space in the reception consists of a series of shelves that can be easily reconfigured, allowing the organization to promote its latest work. These replaced enclosed display cases that were time-consuming to change. The focal "train" and "hedges," linear wooden structures that organize the spaces, are multifunctional. They contain recesses that can

be used as shelving, for display or for storage; sketches can be pinned into them and they conceal cables. The structures form diverse workspaces, such as a glazed private office, phone booth, raised individual desk overlooking the office floor, and both enclosed and open meeting tables.

Robust, self-finished materials—such as wood cladding, and resin-coated plywood countertops, shelving, and cabinets— are used liberally to ensure durability, limit maintenance, and avoid nonessential finishes. The partitions are made of reclaimed wood flooring, which has been sawn down and stacked horizontally or vertically, giving the interior a tactile quality. All new wood and plywood used in the interior is FSC-certified.

The construction methods were chosen to work around the building occupants and take into account the ultimate end of the project. All construction had to be carried out after office hours—a situation that lent itself to quick, dry construction methods, avoiding finishes such as paint that would be wet and release fumes following application. The hedges were prefabricated in manageable sections. Simple construction methods ensure that all components can be easily taken apart for recycling or reuse. This approach results in an honest expression of the construction: for example, in the phone booth, lambswool acoustic insulation shows behind a metal grille that is simply screwed over it.

Below left
The "train" creates a variety of workspaces, including a private office and raised podium, to which these stairs lead. Durable, low-maintenance materials such as self-finished wood are used. Low-energy lightbulbs are suspended over the desk in the office.

Below right
The existing carpet tiles have been rearranged to create a subtle pattern through their differing degrees of wear.

Case study Long-term project 2

Renctas store, Brasilia (Brazil) by Domo Arquitetos Associados

The Renctas store in Brasilia by Domo Arquitetos Associados was created to sell products made by Brazilian artisans. Renctas is a Brazilian nongovernmental organization (NGO) that uses its profits to campaign against illegal trafficking of the country's wildlife.

Serviceable elements of the existing store, comprising the store window, were retained to avoid unnecessary new materials. However, the lighting was replaced with low-energy fixtures to reduce the interior's energy consumption.

The store design alludes to Renctas's environmental mission by showcasing sustainable uses of wood and other natural materials in interior design. One wall is clad in waste wood from a sawmill that processes FSC-certified wood, creating a striking, patterned backdrop to the display shelving. Elsewhere, wallpaper made of renewable vegetable fibers covers a wall and ceiling. All furniture is made of FSC-certified MDF,

made in Brazil with reclaimed and recycled wood, and low formaldehyde content. The textile drape screening the changing room is a naturally dyed fabric embroidered with dried native flowers.

Sustainable man-made materials have not been overlooked. Certified recycled vinyl, formed from plastic waste, provides the floor covering, but is printed to resemble wood.

Above
A striking wall formed of wood waste provides a backdrop to the display shelving. The furniture is made of recycled, certified MDF.

Opposite left
The drape to the changing cubicle is colored with natural dyes and decorated with local dried flowers.

Above
The store sells a variety of products made by Brazilian designers.

Above
Wallpaper made of renewable vegetable fibers covers part of the wall and ceiling.

Below right
The systems were upgraded with low-energy spotlights and strip lighting in the ceiling and display shelving.

Conclusion

We have seen that environmental issues are pressing problems for our generation and for future ones. The issues are not confined to much-touted climate change—which is already beginning to adversely affect our lives and the Earth's ecosystems—but include diminishing resources and biodiversity, waste, human allergies and stress, and water scarcity. Human activity is the primary cause of all of these problems, and human population growth is exacerbating the damage. Luckily, humans are unique in having the intelligence and infrastructure to tackle these problems, for our own sake and for the benefit of other species.

It is apparent that the construction industry and interior design contribute significantly to our impact on the environment. Interior designers can therefore make a valuable difference, both through their design role on projects and their capacity to influence and support the wider design team. This should be seen as a challenge rather than a chore: after all, design is problem-solving and environmental damage is simply another problem that designers must help to solve.

Thankfully, solutions are readily available. Some of these are to be found by relearning lessons from past designers. Traditional building types, such as the igloo and the yurt, reveal seminal passive design principles, such as using daylight, natural ventilation, and insulation. More recently, iconic designers, including Charles Rennie Mackintosh

and the Bauhaus group, demonstrated how to use natural materials, efficient modern construction techniques, and reminders of the value of nature in their interiors. Clearly, the latest technology, materials, and understanding of environmental design give today's designers more options to help create a sustainable project.

We have established that sustainable design is an approach rather than a prescribed aesthetic style. It is about meeting people's needs today while considering those of future generations. Any truly good design is sustainable, as addressing environmental issues is an integral part of a successful design solution.

There are many issues for the interior designer to consider in order to achieve a good design. It is vital to assess the consequences of every design decision and accept that compromises will often be necessary. The best way to ensure rigor in this process is to ask oneself a series of questions that cover all aspects of a project and all stages of its life cycle. This should ascertain the interior's function and expected longevity, and how these might influence which energy and water systems, materials, and construction methods are appropriate, as well as thinking ahead to how the interior will function and what will become of it when it is no longer useful. Opting for one of the many available assessments for sustainable construction is a great way to formalize the design process and benchmark the results against industry standards.

This book has begun to set out the knowledge required to help interior designers choose the most sustainable energy and water systems, materials, and construction methods for their particular project. Evidently, there are clear priorities. For energy, these mean first using passive design, then energy-efficient products, then renewable energy. For water, passive design comes before water-saving products and water reuse and recycling. For materials and construction, the key is to reduce, then reuse, then recycle, then use renewable virgin materials. But the decision-making must be informed by project-specific factors—not least whether the project is seen as temporary, flexible, or long-term.

We have covered the points to look out for when specifying base materials, flooring, finishes, fabrics, furniture, insulation, and adhesives. A wealth of independent guidance and product databases exists to provide more detailed guidance, and help designers avoid any "greenwash." Meanwhile, product certification systems give quantifiable assurance on particular aspects of a product's environmental impact. Details of these are summarized in the Further Reading section.

Other designers' projects are another important resource. The exemplar projects featured here attest that sustainable design can be achieved across a whole range of building sectors, countries, and project types. The results are sophisticated and well-thought-out projects that happen to consider the environment. Not all the projects were designed by interior designers—an indication that there is scope for interior designers to be more active in this market.

We have seen common themes across all the projects, as well as similar approaches within the temporary, flexible, and long-term project categories.

Designers of temporary projects favor reused and recycled materials and simple, lightweight constructions. They necessarily give much thought to the project's end, typically allowing for components to be reused, but are often unable to fully address energy and water use. They generally take a more experimental approach to sustainable design, relishing the opportunity to showcase innovative ideas.

Flexible projects tend to use building systems, materials, and construction methods that facilitate frequent changes. How the space will function is a critical consideration for the designers. Flexibility usually prolongs the longevity of a project, but, in any case, the flexible elements can often easily be removed for reuse or recycling.

Long-term projects typically use robust materials and construction methods that will last, but sometimes justify the use of materials with reasonably high embodied energy. These projects have the strongest focus on addressing energy and water use. The components are typically recyclable at the end of their life, and the sustainable aspects of the design are often hidden and totally integrated in the overall design solution.

The final message is to enjoy the challenge of sustainable design and the opportunity of helping solve perhaps humankind's toughest problem.

Koby Cottage is surrounded by nature and its glazed external walls ensure that the view forms part of the interior.

ENDMATTER

180 GLOSSARY

180 FURTHER READING

182 WEBSITES

186 PICTURE CREDITS

187 INDEX

192 ACKNOWLEDGMENTS

Glossary

The following environmental and technical terms are used within this book and merit explanation:

Adaptable capable of long-term changes.

Biodiversity the variety of living species in the environment.

Biomimicry technology imitating natural systems.

Building/external envelope the external walls, floor, and roof of a building.

Building/external fabric the external materials of a building.

Building systems heating, lighting, ventilation, and cooling systems.

Carbon common abbreviation for carbon dioxide and other greenhouse gases.

Certificate of occupancy when a completed interior is officially given to the client.

Chain of custody record of all stages of a material's production process from source to site.

Climate change changes to average weather patterns caused by global warming.

Cross-ventilation natural air movement from one side of a building to the other.

Embodied energy and water the energy and water needed to create a product.

Fit-out creation of the interior of a new building.

Flexible capable of day-to-day changes.

Formaldehyde gas emitted by some materials that is linked to indoor air pollution and health risks.

Fossil fuels combustible material formed from living matter: coal, oil, and natural gas.

Global warming warming of the Earth linked to excess greenhouse gases produced by human activity.

Greenhouse effect natural process of greenhouse gases keeping the Earth warm.

Greenhouse gases gases in the Earth's atmosphere, including carbon dioxide, methane, ozone, nitrous oxide, and hydrofluorocarbons (HFCs).

Greenwash misleading claim that a product or design is sustainable.

Graywater waste water from washbasins, sinks, baths, and appliances.

Life cycle the stages a product or design goes through before, during, and after a project.

Living roof/living wall wall or roof covered with plants.

Modern methods of construction (MMC) technological building techniques, such as prefabrication.

Nanotechnology technology that operates at a minute scale.

Off-gassing when a material emits gases, such as VOCs, during or after installation.

OSB (Oriented Strand Board) a type of particle board.

Passive design manipulating a building to exploit the natural climate.

Plumbing fixtures bathroom appliances, including baths, washbasins, and toilets.

Potable water clean, drinking water.

Prefabrication constructing components in a factory to be delivered ready-made to site.

Rammed earth construction method using compacted soil to form walls

Sick Building Syndrome symptoms caused by being in an interior with poor air quality.

Specification choosing products.

Stack effect hot air rising.

Sustainability meeting today's needs without compromising future generations' needs.

Thermal mass capacity to store heat or coolness.

U-value measure of thermal performance through external envelope.

VOCs (Volatile Organic Compounds) gases emitted from certain materials and linked to indoor air pollution and health risks.

Further reading

Book and articles

Adam, David, "Explainer: Global Carbon Reduction Targets," *Guardian*, October 7, 2008

Alekett, K. & Campbell, C. J., "The Peak and Decline of World Oil and Gas Production," *Materials and Energy*, vol. 18, no. 1, 2003, pp. 5–20

Alekett, Kjell, "Reserve Driven Forecasts for Oil, Coal and Gas and Limits in Carbon Dioxide Emissions," OECD, Uppsala, 2007

Athena Sustainable Materials Institute, "A Life Cycle Assessment Study of Embodied Effects for Existing Historic Buildings," Athena Sustainable Materials Institute, Ontario, July 14, 2009

Bronwell, Blaine, *Transmaterial 2—A Catalog of Materials that Redefine our Physical Environment*, Princetown Architectural Press, New York, 2008

Brower, Cara, Mallory, Rachel & Ohlman, Zachary, *Experimental Eco Design*, RotoVision SA, Switzerland, 2009

Buxton, Pamela, "Designed for Living," *RIBA Journal*, August/September 2009, pp. 64–65

Carbon Trust, "Building a Brighter Future: A Guide to Low Carbon Building Design," HMSO, London, 2005

Chapagain, A. K., et al, "The Water Footprint of Cotton Consumption," Unesco-IHE, Delft, September 2005

Chiras, Daniel D., *The Natural House—A Complete Guide to Healthy, Energy-Efficient, Environmental Homes*, Chelsea Green Publishing Co., White River Junction, 2000

Contal-Chavannes, Marie-Hélène, Revedin, Jana & Herzog, Thomas, *Sustainable Design: Towards a New Ethic in Architecture and Town Planning*, Birkhauser, Basel, 2009

Crawford, Alan, *Charles Rennie Mackintosh*, Thames & Hudson, London, 1995

Curtis, William J. R., *Modern Architecture Since 1900*, Phaidon Press, London, 1987, 3rd ed.

Dickie, Phil, "Making Water. Desalination: Option or Distraction for a Thirsty World?," WWF International, Gland, June 2007

Dyckhoff, Tom, "Will $1m Help us Turn our Buildings Green?," *Times—The Review*, September 26 2009, p. 7

EcoLiving, "Eco-friendly Interior Design—A Guide to Creating a Sustainable and Ecological Interior," EcoLiving, www.ecological-living.co.uk, 2010

Energy Saving Trust, "Energy-Efficient Ventilation in Dwellings—A Guide for Specifiers," Energy Saving Trust, London, March 2006

Fairs, Marcus & Dixon, Tom, *Green Design: Creative Sustainable Designs for the 21st Century*, Carlton Publishing Group, London, 2009

Frampton, Kenneth, *Modern Architecture: A Critical History*, Thames & Hudson, London, 1992, 3rd ed.

Fuad-Luke, Alastair, *Eco Design Handbook*, Thames & Hudson, London, 2004, 2nd ed.

Gill, Deborah, et al, *Style & Design: 100 Years of Change*, Parragon, Bath, 1998

Griffiths-Sattenspiel, Bevan & Wilson, Wendy, "The Carbon Footprint of Water," River Network, Portland, May 2009

Hewitt, Mike, "Global Metal Reserves," 24 Gold, www.24gold.com, December 1, 2006

HM Government & Sustainability Forum, "Strategy for Sustainable Construction," HM Government, London, June 2008

Hunter, Will, "Design of the Times," *BD Magazine—Interiors*, Issue 30, September 2009, p. 16

IPCC, "Climate Change 2007: Synthesis Report—Summary for Policymakers," Intergovernmental Panel on Climate Change, Geneva, 2007

Jones, Dr. Louise, *Environmentally Responsible Design—Green and Sustainable Design for Interior Designers*, John Wiley & Sons, Hoboken, 2008

Langston, Rowena H. W., "Offshore Wind Farms and Birds: Round 3 Zones, Extensions to Round 1 and Round 2 Sites and Scottish Territorial Waters," RSPB, Sandy, February 2010

McDonough, William & Braungart, Michael, *Cradle to Cradle: Remaking the Way We Make Things*, North Point Press, New York, 2002

The Hannover Principles: Design for Sustainability, William McDonough and Partners, Charlottesville, 1992

McGraw Hill, "Global Green Building Trends: Market Growth and Perspectives from Around the World," McGraw Hill Construction, New York, September 19, 2008

Mumford, Lewis, *The Conduct of Life*, Harcourt, Brace & Company, New York, 1951

NHBC Foundation, "Zero Carbon Compendium: Who's Doing What in Housing Worldwide," PRP Architects, Amersham, 2009

OECD, "OECD Factbook 2010—Economic, Environmental and Social Statistics," OECD, May 25, 2010

"Open," *IDFX Magazine*, February 2010, pp. 9–10

Pagnamenta, Robin, "20,000 people, 192 countries. Welcome to the Carbon Circus," *Times*, October 24, 2009, p. 56

Papanek, Victor, *The Green Imperative: Natural Design for the Real World*, Thames & Hudson, New York, 1995

Pearson, David, *Earth to Spirit—In Search of Natural Architecture*, Gaia Books, London, 2000, 2nd ed.

Pilatowicz, Grazyna, *Eco-Interiors: A Guide to Environmentally Conscious Interior Design*, John Wiley & Sons, New York, 1995

Population Reference Bureau, "2009 World Population Data Sheet," Population Reference Bureau, Washington, August 2009

Population Reference Bureau, "World Population Highlights: Key Findings from PRB's 2008 World Population Data Sheet," Population Reference Bureau, Washington, September 2009

Raconteur, "Building for the Future," *Raconteur Media*, September 22, 2009

Revenga, Carmen & Cassar, Angela, "Freshwater Trends and Projections: Focus on Africa," WWF International, Gland, 2002

Rhodes, Chris, "Short on Reserves: the Planet's Metal Reserves Could Be Running Out Faster Than We Think...," Find Articles, findarticles.com, August 25, 2008

Roaf, Sue, Fuentes, Manuel & Thomas, Stephanie, *Ecohouse: A Design Guide*, Architectural Press, Oxford, 2001

Robinson, Nicole, "Eco Friends," *FX Magazine*, February 2010, pp. 48–51

Sanctuary, "Small Talk," *Sanctuary*, Issue 9, October 10, 2009, p.36

Schildt, Goran, *Alvar Aalto: The Mature Years*, Rizzoli, New York, 1991

Steele, James, *Eames House: Charles and Ray Eames*, Phaidon Press, London, 1994

Sustain, "Energising Development in a Changing Climate," *Sustain*, Issue 31, October 1, 2009

Trocme, Suzanne, *Influential Interiors—Shaping 20th Century Style: Key Interior Designers*, Mitchell Beazley, London, 1999

UN World Commission on Environment and Development, "The Brutland Report: Our Common Future," Oxford University Press, New York, 1987

Weston, Richard, *Alvar Aalto*, Phaidon Press, London, 1995

Wilhide, Elizabeth, *ECO*, Quadrille, London, 2008

Woodman, Ellis, "The Sublime and the Aedicule," *BD*, January 9, 2009, pp. 12–13

Wooley, Tom, et al, *Green Building Handbook: A Companion Guide to Building Products and Their Impact on the Environment*, E & FN Spon, New York, 2000

Websites

The companies listed below do not reflect any endorsement on behalf
of the author or publisher, but are given for information only.

Designers

Andrew Maynard Architects	www.maynardarchitects.com	Australia
Antiques By Design	www.antiquesbydesign.co.uk	UK
Artek	www.artek.fi	International
Blanc, Patrick	www.verticalgardenpatrickblanc.com	France
Bligh Voller Nield	www.bvn.com.au	Australia
Bluarch	www.bluarch.com	US
BroadwayMalyan	www.broadwaymalyan.com	International
Burnt Toast	www.burnttoastdesign.co.uk	UK
Cannon Design	www.cannondesign.com	US, China, India
Carl Turner Architects	www.ct-architects.co.uk	UK
Carr	www.carr.net.au	Australia
Clive Sall Architecture	www.clivesallarchitecture.co.uk	UK
Daniel Becker Design Studio	www.danielbecker.eu	Germany
dARCH Studio	www.darchstudio.com	Greece
David Kohn Architects	www.davidkohn.co.uk	UK
Domo Arquitetos Associados	www.domo.arq.br	Brazil
Dow Jones Architects	www.dowjonesarchitects.com	UK
Garrison Architects	www.garrisonarchitects.com	US
Helicon Works	www.heliconworks.com	US
Herbert & Mason	www.herbertmason.com	Australia
Hurley Palmer Flatt	www.hurleypalmerflatt.com	International
Jestico + Whiles	www.jesticowhiles.com	UK, Czech Republic
Jurica, Jaroslav	www.huberokororo.net	Czech Republic
Kapteinbolt	www.kapteinbolt.nl	Netherlands
Koudenburg, Alrik	www.alrik.nl	Netherlands
Logerot, Aïssa	www.aissalogerot.com	France
Marriott, Michael	www.michaelmarriott.com	UK
Matt Gibson Architecture + Design	www.mattgibson.com.au	Australia
McDonough, William	www.mcdonough.com	US
Mihaly Slocombe Architects	www.mihalyslocombe.com.au	Australia
Molo	www.molodesign.com	Canada
Nendo	www.nendo.jp	Japan, Italy
NoChintz	www.nochintzltd.co.uk	UK
Office of Mobile Design	www.designmobile.com	US
RAU	www.rau.eu	Netherlands
Rawstudio	www.rawstudio.co.uk	UK
Reestore	www.reestore.com	UK
Remodel	www.remodeldesign.co.uk	UK
Ripple Design	www.ripplesite.com	US
Russell, Ryan	www.ryanrussell.com.au	Australia
Samson, Jonas	www.jonassamson.com	Netherlands
Shigeru Ban Architects	www.shigerubanarchitects.com	Japan, US, France

Skylab Architecture	www.skylabarchitecture.com	US
Studio Roosegaarde	www.studioroosegaarde.net	Netherlands
van Bleiswijk, Joost	www.joostvanbleiswijk.com	Netherlands
White Design	www.white-design.co.uk	UK
White + Reid	www.whiteandreid.co.uk	UK
Wilson Brothers	www.benwilsondesign.co.uk	UK

Product guidance

Builder Scrap	www.builderscrap.com	Reclaimed products database
Green Building Source (Oikos)	www.oikos.com	Green specification
Green Industry Resource	www.greenindustryresource.com	Green building products database
Green Product Innovation Institute	www.gpinnovation.org	Low toxicity products database
Greenspec	www.greenspec.co.uk	Green specification
Materia	www.materia.nl	Innovative products database
Mutant Materials	www.mutantmaterials.com	Innovative products database
One Planet Products	www.oneplanetproducts.com	Green products database
Rematerialise	extranet.kingston.ac.uk/rematerialise	Recycled products database
Salvo	www.salvoweb.com	Reclaimed products database
Selector	selector.com/au/sustainable	Green products database
Transmaterial	www.transmaterial.net	Innovative products database
Waste Resources Action Programme	rcproducts.wrap.org.uk	Recycled products database
Whole Building Design Guide	www.wbdg.org/design/greenspec.php	Green specification

Certification bodies

Beam Society	www.beamsociety.org.hk	BEAM assessment
Building Research Establishment	www.bre.co.uk	BREEAM assessment
Carbon Buzz	www.carbonbuzz.org	Post-occupancy analysis
Ecolabel Index	www.ecolabelling.org	Certification database
Forest Stewardship Council	www.fsc.org	Wood certification
German Sustainable Building Council (DGNB)	www.dgnb.de	DGNB assessment
Green Building Council Australia	www.gbca.org.au	Green Star Australia assessment
Green Building Initiative	www.greenglobes.com	Green Globes assessment
GreenGuard	www.greenguard.org	Air quality certification
Indian Green Building Council	www.igbc.in	LEED India assessment
Japan GreenBuild Council	www.ibec.or.jp	CASBEE assessment
McDonough Braungart Design Chemistry	www.mbdc.com	Cradle to Cradle certification
National Australian Building Environmental Rating System	www.nabers.com.au	NABERS assessment
New Zealand Green Building Council	www.nzgbc.org.nz	Green Star New Zealand assessment
Royal Institute of Chartered Surveyors	www.ska-rating.com	Ska Rating
Soil Association	www.soilassociation.org	Organic certification
US Green Building Council	www.usgbc.org	LEED assessment

Sustainability organizations

Aerias	www.aerias.org	Air quality
Athena Institute	athenasmi.org	Sustainable materials

BioRegional	www.bioregional.com	Green building
Carbon Trust	www.carbontrust.co.uk	Carbon reduction
CIRIA	www.ciria.org.uk/suds	Sustainable drainage
Ecological Building Network (EBNet)	www.ecobuildnetwork.org	Green building
Energy Saving Trust	www.energysavingtrust.org.uk	Energy saving
United States Environmental Protection Agency	www.epa.gov	Environment
European Environment Agency	glossary.eea.europa.eu	Environment
Friends of the Earth	www.foe.co.uk	Renewable wood
Greenpeace	www.greenpeace.org.uk	Renewable wood
Intergovernmental Panel on Climate Change	www.ipcc.ch	Climate change
International Initiative for a Sustainable Built Environment	www.iisbe.org	Green building
One Planet Living	www.oneplanetliving.org	Sustainable living
Onsite	onsite.rmit.edu.au	Waste reduction
Plasterboard Sustainability Partnership	www.plasterboardpartnership.org	Sustainable gypsum wall board
Save Water	www.savewater.com.au	Water saving
Sustainable Energy Research Team	www.bath.ac.uk/mech-eng/sert/embodied	Embodied energy
Sustainable Floors	www.sustainablefloors.co.uk	Sustainable flooring
UN Environment Programme	www.unepsbci.org	Environment
Waste Resources Action Programme	www.wrap.org.uk	Recycled products
Waterwise	www.waterwise.org.uk	Water saving
World Business Council for Sustainable Development	www.wbcsd.org	Green building
World Green Building Council	www.worldgbc.org	Green building
York University Environment Department	www.york.ac.uk/depts/eeem	Air quality

Manufacturers

Ash & Embers	www.ashandembers.com	Fireplaces
Auro	www.auro.co.uk	Natural paints
Bottle Alley Glass	www.bottlealleyglass.co.uk	Recycled glass
Brabantia	www.brabantia.com	Clothes airers
Dalsouple	www.dalsouple.com	Rubber
Dimplex	www.dimplex.co.uk	Energy-efficient heating
DIY Kyoto	www.diykyoto.com	Energy meters
Domus	www.domustiles.com	Tiles
Ecoplay	www.ecoplay.nl	Graywater recycling
Graham & Brown	www.grahambrown.com	Wallpaper
Hansgrohe	www.hansgrohe.co.uk	Bathroom ware
Ideal Standard	www.ideal-standard.co.uk	Bathroom ware
InterfaceFLOR	www.interfaceflor.eu	Carpet tiles
Milliken	www.millikencarpet.com	Carpets
Mundy Veneer	www.mundyveneer.com	Veneers
Organic Cotton	www.organiccotton.biz	Cotton
Planet Positive	www.ecokettle.com	Water and energy-saving products
Roca	www.roca-uk.com	Bathroom ware
Royal Mosa	www.mosa.nl	Tiles

Solarcentury	www.solarcentury.com	Solar panels
Straight	www.straight.co.uk	Recycling bins
Victorian Woodworks	www.victorianwoodworks.co.uk	Wood flooring

Sustainable product suppliers

Gecco Interiors	www.geccointeriors.co.uk	Green interior products
Green Building Store	www.greenbuildingstore.co.uk	Green building products
Greenworks	www.greenworks-energy.co.uk	Renewable energy systems
Wolseley Sustainable Building Center	www.wolseleysbc.co.uk	Green building products

Press

Dezeen	www.dezeen.com	Design magazine
Frame	www.framemag.com	Interior design magazine
Great Interior Design	www.greatinteriordesign.com	Interior design blog
Inhabitat	www.inhabitat.com	Sustainable design magazine
School of Interior Design	www.schoolofinteriordesign.org	Interior design articles

Other

Air Quality	www.airquality.co.uk	Air quality resource
Autodesk Ecotect Analysis	www.autodesk.com/ecotect	Energy assessment software
BuildDesk	www.builddesk.co.uk	Energy assessment software
Capital Waste Facts	www.capitalwastefacts.com	Waste data
Children's Furniture	www.childrensfurniture.co.uk	Children's furniture guide
Composting Toilet	compostingtoilet.org	Composting toilet resource
Department for Business Innovation and Skills	www.bis.gov.uk	Government department
Department for Environment, Food and Rural Affairs	www.defra.gov.uk	Government department
Department of Energy and Climate Change	www.decc.gov.uk	Government department
Design Museum London	www.designmuseum.org	Design museum
Ecoartisan	www.ecoartisan.org	Paint resource
Electropaedia	www.mpoweruk.com	Electricity resource
Empire State building	www.esbsustainability.com	Sustainable retrofit
Global Trees Campaign	www.globaltrees.org	Tree resource
Go Wright	www.gowright.org	Frank Lloyd Wright resource
Holistic Interior Designs	www.holistic-interior-designs.com	Sustainable interior design resource
Jumbo Stay	www.jumbostay.com	Hotel chain
Mineral Town	www.mineraltown.com	Geology resource
Natural Environment	www.natural-environment.com	Nature articles database
Peak Oil	www.peakoil.net	Peak oil resource
Recycling Guide	www.recycling-guide.org.uk	Recycling resource
Sustainable Living Directory	www.sustainablelivingdirectory.com	Sustainable living resource
Water Filtering	www.waterfiltering.com	Water quality resource
Wild Again	www.wild-again.org	Reforestation champion
WoodBin	www.woodbin.com	Wood finishes resource
World Nuclear Association	www.world-nuclear.org	Nuclear power resource

Picture credits

T top, L left, R right, C center, B bottom

6 RAU; 7L Elina Droussou/designer: dARCH Studio; 7R John Wheatley/designer: Matt Gibson Architecture + Design; 8 Royal Mosa; 10T, 10B Jon Moxon; 11TL, 11TR, 11BL, 11BR Kathleen Chan; 12T Hakura Horiuchi; 12B Kathleen Chan; 13 Nicholas Hacking; 14 Li Jun; 15 Gayle Babcock, Architectural Imageworks/designer: Cannon Design; 16 CARR; 17T Garrison Architects; 17B Jestico + Whiles; 18TL Philip Sayer; 18TR Siân Moxon; 18CL, 18CR Jestico + Whiles; 18B Siân Moxon; 19L Nicholas Hacking; 19R Ben Forsyth; 20L, 20R Nicholas Hacking; 21 Karen J. Ten Eyck; 22 Wendy Hannan; 23 Ryan Theodore; 24L, 24R Jon Moxon; 25 Maarten Willemstein/designer: Jonas Samson; 26 Angie Seckinger/designer: Bill Hutchins; 27 Emma Cross/designer: Mihaly Slocombe; 28T, 28B Jaroslav Jurica; 30 Marla Aufmuf/designer: Ripple Design; 33T Siân Moxon; 33B Auro; 35 Blink Image/designer: Jestico + Whiles; 36 Siân Moxon; 37 Nicholas Hacking; 39 Vassilis Skopelitis/designer: dARCH Studio; 40T, 40B Sanjay Prasad/designer: NoChintz and Karen Smart; 41T, 41B Zoe Fudge/designer: Clive Sall Architecture and Carl Turner Architects; 42 Sabine Schweigert/designer: Artek; 43 Remodel; 44T Studio Roosegaarde; 44B Ripple Design; 45 Bligh Voller Nield; 46 Remodel; 47 Molo; 48 Cannon Design; 49 Fiodor Sumkin/designer: Alrik Koudenburg and Joost van Bleiswijk; 50L Straight; 50R Emma Cross/designer: Bligh Voller Nield; 51T Kathleen Chan; 51C, 51B Zoe Fudge/designer: Clive Sall Architecture and Carl Turner Architects; 52 Skylab Architecture; 53 Kathleen Chan; 54, 55T, 55BL, 55BR Gayle Babcock, Architectural Imageworks/designer: Cannon Design; 56L Leadership in Energy and Environmental Design (LEED); 56C Building Research Establishment (BRE); 56R Royal Institute of Chartered Surveyors (RICS); 57L National Australian Building Environmental Rating Scheme (NABERS); 57C Green Building Council Australia (GBCA); 57R Green Building Initiative; 58L Building Environmental Assessment Method (BEAM); 58C Comprehensive Assessment System for Building Environmental Efficiency (CASBEE); 58R German Sustainable Building Council (DGNB); 59TL, 59TR, 59B Emma Cross/designer: Bligh Voller Nield; 60TL, 60TR, 60CL, 60CR, 60B Hurley Palmer Flatt; 61T, 61B Matt Livey/designer: BroadwayMalyan; 62 Siân Moxon; 65 Basil Gloo; 66 Energy Saving Trust; 67L Joachim Baam/designer: Alrik Koudenburg and Joost van Bleiswijk; 67TR Siân Moxon; 67BR Solarcentury; 68TL, 68TR, 68B Jestico + Whiles; 69T, 69B Nicholas Hacking; 70 Nicholas Hacking; 71T Patrick Blanc; 71B Nicholas Hacking; 72 Daniel Becker Design Studio; 73L Dimplex; 73C DIY Kyoto; 73R Brabantia; 75T Ash & Embers; 75B Siân Moxon; 76TL, 76TR Lawrence Anderson/designer: Ripple Design; 76B Marla Aufmuf/designer: Ripple Design; 77 Marla Aufmuf/designer: Ripple Design; 79L Siân Moxon; 79TR Hansgrohe; 79BR Roca; 81TL Hansgrohe; 81 Row2L, 81 Row 3, 81TR Ideal Standard; 81B Product Creation Ltd; 82 Ecoplay; 83L Waterwise; 83R Kathleen Chan; 84 P. Wayne Nalbandian; 85 Lipman; 86TL, 86TR, 86BL, 86BR Royal Mosa; 87T, 87C, 87B Royal Mosa; 88TL, 88TR, 88BL, 88BR InterfaceFLOR; 89TL, 89TR, 89B InterfaceFLOR; 91TL White + Reid; 91TR Victorian Woodworks; 91BL, 91BR Siân Moxon; 93 Kathleen Chan; 94 Jestico + Whiles; 95 Reestore; 96 Reestore; 97L Domus; 97R Siân Moxon/designer: Moxon Cincotta; 98 Molo; 99T, 99C, 99BL, 99BR Molo; 100T Kathleen Chan; 100CL One Planet Living; 100CR McDonough Braungart Design Chemistry (MBDC); 100BL Soil Association; 100BR Forest Stewardship Council (FSC) © 1996 FSC A.C.; 101C Forest Stewardship Council (FSC); 101B Kathleen Chan; 102L Siân Moxon; 102R Bottle Alley Glass; 103TL Mundy; 103TR Kathleen Chan/ manufacturer: Dalsouple; 103BL Milliken; 103BR Siân Moxon; 104L Auro; 104R Graham & Brown; 105 The Organic Textile Company; 106 Guy Chenevix-Trench, Antiques By Design & Contemporary Antiques; 107 CARR; 108 John Wheatley/designer: Matt Gibson Architecture + Design; 109 Lawrence Anderson/designer: Ripple Design; 110L Jestico + Whiles; 110R Emma Cross/designer: Mihaly Slocombe; 111 Andrew Maynard Architects; 112T Garrison Architects; 112B ModCell Ltd/designer: White Design; 113 David Ryle/designer: Wilson Brothers; 114T Aleš Jungmann/designer: Jestico + Whiles; 114B Diana Snape/designer: Ryan Russell; 115 Lioba Schneider/designer: Jumbo Stay; 116TL Rawstudio; 116BL, 116R Nick Rawcliffe/designer: Rawstudio; 117L, 117R Michael Marriott; 118T, 118CL, 118CC, 118CR, 118B Véronique Huyghe/designer: Aïssa Logerot; 119T all sketches Aïssa Logerot; 119BL, 119CR, 119BR Véronique Huyghe/designer: Aïssa Logerot; 120L, 120R Kapteinbolt; 121TL, 121TR, 121B Kapteinbolt; 122 Daici Ano/designer: Nendo; 124 Sanjay Prasad/designer: Nochintz and Karen Smart; 125 Sabine Schweigert/designer: Artek; 126T Michael Marriott Architects; 126B Li Jun/designer: Shigeru Ban Architects; 127T Loana Marinescu/designer: David Kohn Architects; 127B Ben Glazer/designer: Herbert & Mason; 128 Sabine Schweigert/designer: Artek; 129L Ben Glazer/designer: Hebert & Mason; 129R Loana Marinescu/designer: David Kohn Architects; 130 Ben Glazer/ designer: Herbert & Mason; 131T Yasunori Harano/designer: Shigeru Ban Architects; 131B Sabine Schweigert/designer: Artek; 132 Yasunori Harano/designer: Shigeru Ban Architects; 133 Michael Marriott Architects; 134 Joachim Baam/designer: Alrik Koudenburg and Joost van Bleiswijk; 135TL, 135TR, 135B Joachim Baam/designer: Alrik Koudenburg and Joost van Bleiswijk; 136T, 136B Vassilis Skopelitis/designer: dARCH Studio; 137T, 137B Vassilis Skopelitis/designer: dARCH Studio; 138 Burnt Toast; 139 John Wheatley/designer: Matt Gibson Architecture + Design; 140 Dave Lauridsen/designer: Office of Mobile Design; 141T David Ryle/designer: Wilson Brothers; 141B Jeremy Bitterman/designer: Skylab Architecture; 142 Dave Lauridsen/designer: Office of Mobile Design; 143T Jeremy Bitterman/designer: Skylab Architecture; 143B Dave Lauridsen/designer: Office of Mobile Design; 144BL Dave Lauridsen/designer: Office of Mobile Design; 144BR Burnt Toast; 145 David Ryle/designer: Wilson Brothers; 146 David Ryle/designer: Wilson Brothers; 147L, 147R John Wheatley/designer: Matt Gibson Architecture + Design; 148T John Wheatley/designer: Matt Gibson Architecture + Design; 148B Jeremy Bitterman/designer: Skylab Architecture; 149T Dave Lauridsen/Office of Mobile Design; 149B Jeremy Bitterman/designer: Skylab Architecture; 150 Marcus Ginns/designer: Jestico + Whiles; 151T, 151B Marcus Ginns/designer: Jestico + Whiles; 152T, 152BL, 152BR Remodel; 153 Remodel; 154 ModCell Ltd/designer: White Design; 155T Daici Ano/designer: Nendo; 155B David Grandorge/designer: Dow Jones Architects; 156T Antropia/designer: RAU; 156B Garrison Architects; 157 Shannon McGrath/designer: Matt Gibson Architecture + Design; 158TL, 158TR, 158B Daan Roosegaarde/designer: Studio Roosegaarde; 159 Ado/designer: Bluarch; 160T ModCell Ltd/designer: White Design; 160B Shannon McGrath/designer: Matt Gibson Architecture + Design; 161 Daici Ano/designer: Nendo; 162 RAU; 163 Boon Edam/designer: RAU; 164 RAU; 165T, 165B Shannon McGrath/designer: Matt Gibson Architecture + Design; 166 Garrison Architects; 167 Ado/designer: Bluarch;168 Shannon McGrath/designer: Matt Gibson Architecture + Design; 169T David Grandorge/designer: Dow Jones Architects; 169B ModCell Ltd/designer: White Design; 170L David Grandorge/designer: Dow Jones Architects; 170R Ado/designer: Bluarch; 171 David Grandorge/designer: Dow Jones Architects; 172T, 172B Dennis Gilbert/designer: Clive Sall Architecture & Carl Turner Architects; 173L, 173R Dennis Gilbert/designer: Clive Sall Architecture and Carl Turner Architects; 174 Frank Carvalho/designer: Domo Arquitetos Associados; 175TL, 175TR, 175BL, 175BR Frank Carvalho/designer: Domo Arquitetos Associados; 176 Garrison Architects; 178 John Wheatley/designer: Matt Gibson Architecture + Design

Index

Page numbers in *italics* refer to picture captions

A
Aalto, Alvar 22–3
Aalto Stool 60
acetate 105
acrylic 104, 105
adhesives 13, 85, *89,* 94, 109, 113, 115
air-conditioning 73, 77, 142
air-tightness 70, 75
allergies 10, 12, 13, 176
aluminum 90, 102
Andrew Maynard Architects *111*
Antiques by Design *106*
appliances 16, 25, 73, 80
Art Nouveau 21
Artek *42, 125, 129*
Artek exhibit, Milan Furniture Fair *42,* 125, 127, 128, 130, *131,* 133
Arts and Crafts movement 21, 22
assessment process 60–1
assessment systems 53–9, 75, 78, 83, 100–1
asthma 12, 13, 85
Athena Institute 100
Australia
  assessment and certification systems 57, 59, 75, 83, 101
  carbon and greenhouse gas emissions *10,* 11, 24
  projects
    Barrow House, Melbourne *111*
    The Bombed Maché store, Melbourne 125, 127, 129, 130, 131, 132, 133
    Country Victoria House, Kilmore *16, 107*
    Elwood Clothing office, Melbourne 156, 160, 164, *165,* 167, 168, 170
    Green Building Council headquarters, Sydney *45, 59*
    H + B Fashion store, Victoria *114*
    Hill House, Merricks *27, 110*
    Incubation, Melbourne *7, 109, 138,* 142, 144, 147, 148, 149
  water scarcity 13, 78

B
bamboo *7,* 25, 32, *33,* 97, 103, 144, 167
Bauhaus 22, 23, 177
BEAM assessment system 58
biodiversity 10, 12, 13, 25, 32, 84, 176, 180
biomass 74, *75*
biomimicry *89,* 102, 180
Blanc, Patrick *71*

Bleiswijk, Joost van *49,* 134–5
Bligh Voller Nield (BVN) *45, 59*
The Box Project, 100% Design Exhibition, London *40, 125,* 127, 128, 129, 130, 131, 132, 133
Brazil: Renctas store, Brasilia 174–5
BREEAM assessment system 56
brick 22, 46, 69
  in flexible projects 145
  in long-term projects 164, *165,* 168
  reduce 93, 110, 113
  reuse 95, 107, *114*
BroadwayMalyan 60–1
Builder Scrap 114
building envelope 15, 29, 69, 70, 180
building systems 73, 77, 180 *see also* heating systems; lighting; ventilation
Burnt Toast *138,* 144

C
Cannon Design *15, 48,* 54–5
Carbon Buzz 75
carbon emissions 10, 11, 13, 15, 24, 25, 64, 85, 180
cardboard
  corrugated *47,* 113, 137
  in flexible projects *138,* 144, 147, 149
  in furniture construction *47,* 106
  in temporary projects *7, 126, 127,* 129, *130,* 131, 133, 134, 137
Carl Turner Architects *40, 51,* 172–3
carpets 88–9, *91,* 103, 173
Carr *16, 107*
CASBEE assessment system 58
cement board 102
ceramics 85, 86–7, 100, 167
certification systems 53, 75, 83, 86, 100, 101, 177
China
  assessment systems 58
  carbon emissions *10,* 11
  Chengdu Hualin Elementary School 125, *126,* 128, 129, 131, 132
chrome 102
climate change 10–11, 13, 24–5, 29, 64, 78, 84, 176, 180
Clive Sall Architecture *40, 51,* 172–3
Cloud Softlight (Molo) 98
concrete 23, 69, 90, *91,* 97, *109,* 110, 168
construction industry
  environmental impact 10, 13, 14, 18, 29, 32, 64, 176
  sustainable approach 14–16, 64
construction methods
  connectors *47,* 109, 115, 131, 134, 147

energy consumption 13, 15, *18,* 19–20, 32, 64, 69, 107, 177
environmental impact 13, 32, 64, 107–8
flat-packed 109, *125,* 130
flexible projects 109, 145, 147, *177*
health issues 109, 113
long-term projects 109, 111, 168, 173,177
modern methods of construction (MMC) 109, 168, 180
modular construction *107,* 111, *112,* 113, *141,* 147, 168, 171
"pop-up" interiors 125, *126,* 132
recycle 109, 115, 171, 173
reduce 110–11, 113
in renovation projects 110, 114, 145, 168
and resource consumption 13, 107, 111, 113
reuse 109, 114–15, 133, 137, 171
sustainable approach 25, 26, 37, 47–8, 52, 64, 109–15
temporary projects 109, 130–1, 177
and thermal performance 15, 64, 69, 107, 109, 110–11, 114, 150, 162
  see also insulation
traditional 19–20, 21, 22, 23, 26, 27, 109, 176
waste issues 13, *18,* 64, 85, 107, 109, 113, 114
water consumption *18,* 109
  see also furniture construction; prefabrication
cork 93, 97, 103, 110, 144
cotton 85, 94, 101, 103, 105
"cradle to cradle" 36, 86, 100

D
Daniel Becker Design Studio *72*
dARCH Studio *7, 39,* 136–7
DGNB assessment system 58
Domo Arquitetos Associados 174–5
Dow Jones Architects *155*
Drawerment (Jurica) *28*

E
Eames, Charles and Ray 23
eco style 26–7
Ecoartisan 104
electricity *44,* 64, 65, *67,* 74, 88, 158, *163*
  see also hydroelectricity
Eleftheriades, Yiorgos 137
energy systems
  assessments 75

and construction methods 13, 15, *18*, *19–20*, 32, 64, 69, 107, 177
cost issues 33
energy efficiency 19, 25, 66, 72–3, 77, 142, 158, 162, 177 *see also under* lighting; ventilation
energy labels 75
environmental impact 13, *18*, 29, 32, 36, 64–5
flexible projects 66, 142
long-term projects 66, 158, 160, 162–3, 177
low-energy design 66–7, 70, 76–7 *see also under* lighting
in material production 25, 32, 84–5, 90, 93, 94, 102–3, 104, 180
and passive design 19–20, 64, 66, 68–71, 75, 142, 162, 177
renewable systems 25, 33, 44, 65, 66, 74, 77, 162–3, 177
and renovation projects 15, 66, 69, 74, 162
and resource consumption 64, 65, 74, *75*
sustainable approach 15, 25, 37, 41, 44, 64, 66–77, 177
temporary projects 66, 128, 177
and water supply 12–13, 64, 78
see also electricity
EU Energy Label Scheme 75
exhibitions 42, 98–9, 125, 131 *see also* Artek exhibit; Box Project; Kiosk store
Extensions range (Aïssa Logerot) 118–19

F
fabrics
certification systems 101, 174
environmental impact 85, 105
natural 21, 85, 105
sustainable approach 94, 98, 105, 171, 174
synthetic 105, 174
felt 20, 103, 105, 127
fiberboard 102, 144 *see also* MDF
finishes
assessment systems 100
environment impact 12, 50, 85, 90, 94
health issues 12, 13, 16, 85, 109
natural 33, 104
sustainable approach 45, 46, 93, 94, 104
synthetic 104
Finland: Säynätsälo Town Hall 22–3
fit-outs 39, 53, 78, 126, 140, 149, 155, 180
flooding and flood protection 66, 78, 83
flooring
assessment systems 100
life cycles 88–9
natural *88*, 103, 164
recycle *91*, 103, 144, 167

sustainable approach 27, *91*, 103–4, 144, 173
synthetic 103
Forest Stewardship Council (FSC) 101, 173, 174
formaldehyde 52, 94, 102, 104, 144, 174, 180
fossil fuels 10, *11*, 12, 64, 78, 97, 111, 180
France: Natural History Museum, Toulouse *71*
furniture construction
connectors *116*, 117, 120
flat-packed 116, 117, 118–19, 120–1
mass production 22, 23, 120
modular construction 98, *99*, 145
recycle 118, 174
sustainable approach 116–21
furniture materials
environmental impact 12, 106
flexibility *42, 49*, 98
natural 98, 106
reuse *28, 39*, 106, 137
sustainable approach *28, 49*, 52, 98–9, 106, 144

G
Garrison Architects *17, 112, 156*
gas 12, 64, 65
Germany
assessment systems 58
Bauhaus school director's office, Dessau 22
carbon emissions 10, 11, *24*
glass 22, 54, *68, 97*, 102, *152*, 162, 171
Global Ecolabelling Network 75, 83, 101
global warming 73, 78, 111, 180 *see also* climate change
Good Wood Guides 97
Greece: Yeshop fashion boutique, Athens *7, 39*, 136–7
Green Dot system 101
Green Globes assessment system 57
Green Guide to Specification (BRE) 100
Green Product Innovation Institute 94, 106
Green Star Australia assessment system 57, 59
Green Star New Zealand assessment system 57
GreenGuard 94, 101, 106
greenhouse gas emissions 10, 11, 12–13, 24, 64, 85, 180
"greenwash" 27, 90, 100, 177, 180
Gropius, Walter 22
gypsum wall board 46, *97*, 103, 113, 137

H
hanging chair (Rawstudio) 116–17
health issues 10, 176
and construction methods 109, 113
finishes 12, 13, 16, 85, 109
materials 12, 13, 25, 84, 85, 90, 144
water systems 13
heating systems 19, 20, 44, 73, 74, *75*, 77, 142, 162
hemp 94, 97, 105, 111
Herbert & Mason *127*
hessian 103, 105
Hong Kong 58
Hurley Palmer Flatt 60–1
Hutchins, Bill (Helicon Works) *26*
hydroelectricity 65, *86*

I
igloos 19, 176
India
assessment systems 56
carbon emissions *10*, 11
insulation 46, 69, 77, 90, 110–11, 150, *154*, 162, 167
InterfaceFLOR 88–9
interior design and designers
and architects 29, 34, 53, 66, 78
assessment systems 37, 53–61
compromises 32–4
consequences, foreseeing 36–7
environmental impact *18*, 29, 32, 176
history, learning from 19–23, 176
key questions 38–9, 41–52, 92, 177
life cycle approach 27, 36–7, 38, 177
preconceptions, disregarding 26–7
project team relationships 34

J
Japan
assessment systems 58
Moss House, Tokyo 155, 160, *161*, 170
Jestico + Whiles *34, 68, 114*, 150–1
Jurica, Jaroslav (Hubero Kororo Design Group) *28*

K
Kapteinbolt 120–1
Kiosk store, London Design Festival 125, *126*, 128, 129, 130, 131, 133
Kohn, David *127*
Koudenberg, Alrik *49*, 134–5

L
leather 22, 23, 105
LEED assessment system 54–5, 56
LEED India 56
Life Cycle Assessments or Analyses (LCAs) 37
life cycles

defined 180
materials 37, 64, 84, 85, 86–9, 90, 93, 100
projects 18, 27, 36–7, 38
lightbulbs 33, 65, *67,* 128
lighting
  energy-efficient *67, 72,* 128, 134, 137, 142, 158
  LED *44, 72,* 98, *99,* 150, 156, 158, 170
  light-emitting wallpaper *25*
  low-energy 32, *67, 72,* 98, *126,* 142, 150, 162, 174 *see also* lightbulbs
  natural 22, 23, *67,* 71, 142, *143,* 160, *161,* 170
  reuse *106,* 142
linoleum 85, 103
living walls 59, 68, 71, 80, 180
Logerot, Aïssa 118–19
Loos, Adolf 23
Lutyens, Sir Edwin 21

M

Mackintosh, Charles Rennie 21, 176–7
Malay houses 19, 20
Marriott, Michael 117, *126*
Materia 102, 106
materials
  assessment 100–1
  base materials 102–3
  certification systems 86, 100, 101
  cost issues 33, 37
  and embodied energy 25, 32, 84–5, 90, 93, 95, 102–3, 104, 180
  embodied water 85, 90, 93, 95, 180
  environmental impact 12, 13, *18,* 32, 36, 64, 84–5, 90, 102
  flexible projects 90, 144, 177
  health issues 13, 84, 85, 90, 144
  for insulation 69, 90, 110–11, 162
  life cycles 37, 64, 84, 85, 86–9, 90, 93, 100
  local 19, 20, 21, 22, 25
  long-term projects 90, 164, 167, 177
  maintenance issues 84, 86, *87, 89,* 90, 93, 158, 164, 173
  natural 19–23, 52, 84–5, *91,* 94, *97,* 102, 164
  reclaimed *see under* reuse
  recycle 36, 52, 90, 91, 96–7, 98, 106, 149, 177 *see also under* flooring; packaging materials
  reduce 90, 91, 93–4, 95, 177
  renewable 25, 84, *88,* 90, 91, 97, 177
  for renovation projects 41, 90, 95
  and resource consumption 12, 13, 25, 29, 84, 90, 96, 104, 105
  reuse *7, 26,* 36, 41, 52, 91, 95–6, 149, 177
  salvage *see under* reuse

sample boards *17*
selecting 37, 41, 42, 43, 45–6, 52, 98–9, 102–6, 177
specifications 90, 91, 92, 180
sustainable approach 13, 25, *27,* 32, 45–6, 52, 64, 86–103
synthetic 45, 52, 90, 97 *see also* plastics
temporary projects 90, 129, 177
transporting 12, 13, *18,* 32, 84, 93, 94, 107
waste issues *18,* 36, 85, 90, 93, 95, 103, 104, 105
see also construction methods; fabrics; finishes; flooring; furniture materials; packaging materials
Matt Gibson Architecture + Design *7, 109, 138, 156*
MDF (medium-density fiberboard) 52, 102, 134, 174
metals 84, 93, 102 *see also* aluminum; steel
methane emissions 10, *11,* 12
Mies van der Rohe, Ludwig 23
Mihaly Slocombe Architects *27, 110*
mirrors 21, 160, *161*
Modernist design 19, 21–3
Molo *47,* 98–9
Mutant Materials 102, 106

N

NABERS assessment system 57
nanotechnology 102, 180
Nendo *155*
Netherlands
  Club Watt, Rotterdam *44,* 156, 158, 162, 163, 170
  Nature Café La Porte, Amsterdam *7,* 156, 162–3, 164
  Nothing advertising agency, Amsterdam *49,* 134–5
New Zealand: assessment systems 57, 75
90° Furniture range (Kapteinbolt) 120–1
NoChintz *40, 125*
nomadic tents 19, 20 *see also* yurts
nuclear power 64
nylon 103, 105

O

off-gassing 12, 85, 180
Office of Mobile Design *140,* 144
One Planet Living 100
OSB (oriented strand board) 102, *125,* 129, 137, *138,* 144, 147, 180

P

packaging materials
  in flexible projects *138,* 144
  recycle *87,* 92, 93, 101, 129
  reduce 93

reuse 129, 132, 133, 137, 144
  in temporary projects *7,* 129, 130
paints 13, 25, 33, 90, 104
paper 20, *87,* 98, 111 *see also* cardboard; wallpaper
particle boards 102 *see also* OSB
partitions 107, 109, 113, 160, 173
passive design 176
  defined 19, 68, 180
  and energy systems 19–20, 64, 66, 68–71, 75, 142, 162, 177
  and renovation projects 39, 162
  and water systems 44, 78, 79, 80, 82, 83, 177
Passivhaus environmental standard 24
photovoltaic panels 33, *67, 74, 77,* 163
plaster *26,* 93, 104
plastics 12, 25, 52, 84, 97, 106, *126,* 129
plumbing fixtures 54, 78, 80, *81, 82,* 163, 180
plywood 102, 116, 129, 130, 145, 173
Poland: Andels Manufaktura hotel, Lodz *114*
pollution 12, *18,* 32, 84, 90
  air 12, 64, 73, 85, 93, 94, 102, 103
  water 78, 80, 85, 94, 103, 105
polyester 103, 105
polypropylene 103, 105
population growth 10, 13, *78,* 176
Prairie School 22
prefabrication
  defined 180
  flexible projects *140*
  in furniture construction 120
  in history of design 22, 23
  long-term projects *112, 140, 156, 168, 169,* 173
  in sustainable approach 25, 64, 90, *107,* 109, *112,* 113
product life cycles 64, 84, 86–9, 93
project teams 34, 78
projects
  adaptable 42, 43, 66, 180
  construction method selection 47–8, 52, 177
  demolition 15, *18,* 36, 42, 52, 85, 95, 107, 109
  duration 42–3, 44, 52, 66, 78, 90, 128, 142, 158
  energy system selection 37, 41, 44, 66, 128, 177
  environmental impact *18,* 36–7
  flexible 42–3, *49,* 52, 66, 90, 109, 140–53, 177, 180
  functioning of the space *27,* 49–51, 132, 148, 156, 170, 173, 177
  heating system selection 44
  life cycles *18, 27,* 36–7, 38
  long-term 42, 43, 52, 66, 90, 109, 111,

155–75, 177
maintenance issues 36, 49
material selection 37, 41, 42, 43, 45–6, 52, 177
new-build 15, 16, 29, 53, 77, 90, 155, 162, 168 see also fit-outs
purpose 39, 41, 125, 127, 140–1, 155–6
redundancy issues 36, 52, 85, 132, 134, 149, 171, 177
temporary 42, 52, 58, 66, 90, 109, 125–37, 177
water system selection 37, 41, 44, 128, 177
see also renovation projects

R
rammed-earth construction 27, 69, 110, 180
RAU architects 7, 156, 162
Rawstudio 116–17
rayon 105
reclamation see reuse
recycle
  and construction methods 109, 115, 171, 173
  flooring 91, 103, 144, 167
  and furniture construction 118, 174
  materials 36, 52, 90, 91, 96–7, 98, 106, 149, 177 see also under flooring; packaging materials
  packaging 87, 92, 93, 101, 129
  and water systems 25, 64, 78, 79, 80, 82, 83, 177
reduce
  in construction methods 110–11, 113
  material use 90, 91, 93–4, 95, 177
Reestore 95, 96
Rematerialise 97, 106
Remodel 42, 46, 152–3
renewables
  energy systems 25, 33, 44, 65, 66, 74, 77, 162–3, 177
  materials 25, 84, 88, 90, 91, 97, 177
renovation projects
  assessment systems 53, 54–5, 56, 57, 58
  construction methods 110, 114, 145, 168
  energy systems 15, 66, 69, 74, 162
  flexible projects 140, 145, 149
  long-term projects 155, 162, 168
  material selection 41, 90, 95
  passive design 39, 162
  in sustainable approach 14–15, 34, 39, 41, 66
  temporary projects 127, 137
  and water systems 15, 78
resource consumption
  and construction methods 13, 107, 111,

113
  and energy systems 64, 65, 74, 75
  environmental impact 10, 12, 13, 29, 32, 176
  and materials 12, 13, 25, 29, 84, 90, 96, 104, 105
reuse
  bricks 95, 107, 114
  and construction methods 109, 114–15, 133, 137, 171
  furniture materials 28, 39, 106, 137
  lighting 106, 142
  materials 7, 26, 36, 41, 52, 91, 95–6, 149, 177
  packaging 129, 132, 133, 137, 144
  and water systems 25, 64, 78, 79, 80, 82, 83, 177
  wood 26, 91, 103, 144, 149, 164, 165, 167, 173
Ripple Design 44, 76–7, 109
Roman baths 19
Royal Mosa 86–9
rubber 91, 97, 101, 103, 104, 144
Russell, Ryan 114

S
salvage see reuse
Salvo 96, 114
Samson, Jonas 25
Scandinavian style 22
seagrass 91, 103
sealants 54, 94, 104, 109
Shigeru Ban Architects 126
Sick Building Syndrome 12, 85, 180
Ska Rating assessment system 56–7, 60–1
Skylab Architecture 52, 141
slate 84
Smart, Karen 125
Soft range (Molo) 47, 98–9
solar gain 68, 71, 77
solar power 65, 66, 68, 74, 77, 163
solar shading 66, 68
South Korean houses 19, 20
Sparks LED light fixtures 72
steel 109, 112, 145, 147, 149, 167, 168
stone 12, 20, 84, 94, 103
straw 26, 102, 112, 162, 167, 168, 169
stress 10, 12, 176
Studio Roosegaarde 44, 158
sustainability, defined 14, 177, 180
Sustainable Energy Research Team, Bath 93
Sustainable Floors 104
Sustainable Urban Drainage Systems (SUDS) 80, 83
Sweden: Jumbo Stay, Stockholm 115

T
thermal insulation see insulation
thermal mass 20, 27, 68, 69, 71, 77, 90, 110, 180
tiles
  carpet 88–9, 173
  ceramic 85, 86–7, 100, 167
  glass 97
Transmaterial 102, 106
transportation and the environment 12, 13, 18, 32, 64, 84, 93, 94, 107
Trench, Guy 106

U
UK
  assessment systems 56–7, 60–1, 75
  carbon emissions 10, 13, 15, 24
  projects
    Auckland House, Swindon 60–1
    BaleHaus, Bath 112, 154, 155, 160, 162, 167, 168, 169, 170, 171
    Design Council headquarters, London 40, 51, 172–3
    The Elgar Room, Royal Albert Hall, London 150–1
    Flash restaurant, Royal Academy of Arts, London 125, 127, 128, 129, 131, 133
    Garden Museum, London 155, 162, 164, 167, 168, 169, 170, 171
    House for the Future, Cardiff 68
    Howies store, Bristol 42, 46, 152–3
    Malmaison Oxford Castle, Oxford 34
    Nike 1948 store, London 113, 140–1, 142, 144, 145, 147, 148, 149
    Smithfield store, Manchester 138, 142, 144, 147, 148, 149
    Willow Tea Rooms, Glasgow 21
    see also Box Project; Kiosk store
US
  assessment systems 56, 57, 75
  carbon emissions 10, 11, 15, 24
  projects
    Country School Prefab, Valley Village 140, 141, 142, 143, 144, 147, 148,149
    Courtyard House, Los Angeles 44, 76–7, 109
    Eames House, Los Angeles 23
    Empire State Building, New York 15
    Greenhouse nightclub, New York 158, 163, 167, 170, 171
    Hutchins house, Takoma Park, Washington, D.C. 26
    Koby Cottage, Albion 17, 112, 155, 156, 162, 163, 164, 167, 168, 170, 171, 177
    North office, Portland 52, 141, 142,

143, 145, 147, 148, 149
  Oak Park, Chicago 22
  Power House, St. Louis *15, 48,* 54–5
 water scarcity 13
user manuals 51

V
varnishes 90, 93, 94, *97,* 104
ventilation
  cross ventilation 20, 70, 142, *143,* 180
  energy-efficient 59, *73, 77,* 162
  natural 13, 19, 20, 25, 70, 142
  stack ventilation 19, 20, 70, *71, 77,* 180
vernacular design 19–20, 21
vinyl 103, 104, 106, 167, 174
volatile organic compounds (VOCs) 13,
  16, 85, 94, 104, 109, 180

W
wallpaper *25,* 102, 104, *137,* 170, 174
waste issues
  and construction methods 13, *18,* 64,
    85, 107, 109, 113, 114
  environmental impact 10, 12, 13, *18,*
    29, 32, 36, 85, 176
  and materials *18,* 36, 85, 90, 93, 95,
    103, 104, 105
  see also recycle; reduce; reuse
Waste Resources Action Programme
  (WRAP) 97, 106

water meters 80, *81*
water systems
  assessments 78, 83
  and construction methods *18,* 109
  drainage 78, 80
  and energy consumption 12–13, 64, 78
  environmental impact 12–13, *18,* 32,
    36, 64, 78
  flexible projects 142
  graywater 25, 59, 64, 78, 82, 180
  health issues 13
  long-term projects 78, 83, 158, 163, 177
  in material production 85, 90, 93, 95,
    180
  and passive design 44, 78, 79, 80, 82,
    83, 177
  recycle 25, 64, 78, 79, 80, 82, *83,* 177
  and renovation projects 15, 78
  reuse and recycling 25, 64, 78, 79, 80,
    82, *83,* 177
  scarcity issues 10, 12–13, 64, 78, 176
  sustainable approach 15, 25, 37, 41, 44,
    64, 78–83
  temporary projects 128, 177
  water conservation 64, 78, 79, 80, *81,*
    177
  water efficiency 54, 78, 79, 80, 83
Waterwise 83
White Design *112, 154*
Wilson Brothers *113, 141*

wind power 65, 74, 163
wood
  certification systems 101, 173, 174
  reuse *26, 91,* 103, 144, 149, 164, *165,*
    167, 173
  sustainable use 16, 25, 84, *91, 93, 97,*
    174
  wooden boards 102
wool 69, 94, 97, 103, 105, 110
Wright, Frank Lloyd 22

X
XYZ exhibition (Michael Marriott) 117

Y
yurts 19, 20, 176

Acknowledgments

The author wishes to thank all contributors, colleagues, friends, family, and contacts who helped the book happen through their input and support. Special thanks go to Lucy Porter, who developed the concept for the book based on her teaching program for The Glasgow School of Art, Kathleen Chan for managing the images and contributing many illustrations, Jon Moxon, Nick Hacking, Andy Costa, Heinz Richardson, and Jestico + Whiles.

ALL ABOUT

PIANO

A FUN AND SIMPLE GUIDE TO PLAYING KEYBOARD

SPECIAL CD INCLUDES 74 TRACKS
FEATURING LOTS OF GREAT SONGS!

by Mark Harrison

ISBN-13: 978-1-4234-0816-1
ISBN-10: 1-4234-0816-0

HAL•LEONARD®
CORPORATION

7777 W. BLUEMOUND RD. P.O. BOX 13819 MILWAUKEE, WI 53213

Visit Hal Leonard Online at **www.halleonard.com**